Contracts for
YOUR
Business

A straightforward guide to contracts and legal agreements

Charles Boundy

bw

brightword

A Brightword book
www.brightwordpublishing.com

HARRIMAN HOUSE LTD
3A Penns Road
Petersfield
Hampshire
GU32 2EW
GREAT BRITAIN

Tel: +44 (0)1730 233870
Fax: +44 (0)1730 233880
Email: enquiries@harriman-house.com
Website: www.harriman-house.com

First published in Great Britain in 2012

Copyright © Charles Boundy (2012)

The right of Charles Boundy to be identified as the Author has been asserted in accordance with the Copyright, Design and Patents Act 1988.

ISBN: 9781908003218

British Library Cataloguing in Publication Data

A CIP catalogue record for this book can be obtained from the British Library.

Printed and bound in the UK by the CPI Group (UK) Ltd, Chippenham.

THIS BOOK IS DEDICATED TO THAT OTHER
GROWING BUSINESS – MY FAMILY

Get the eBook of

Contracts for

YOUR

Business

for free

As a buyer of the printed version of this book you can download the electronic version free of charge.

To get hold of your copy of the eBook, simply point your smartphone camera at the code above (or go to **ebooks.harriman-house.com/contracts**).

Contents

About the Author   **ix**

Preface   **xi**

Introduction   **1**

CHAPTER 1 Contract Basics   **7**

1.1 What is a contract?   9

1.2 What about the need for agreement?   9

1.3 Clarity and certainty – what happens if everything is not clear?   11

1.4 I understand price but what is 'consideration'?   12

1.5 Legal commitment   12

1.6 When do I need to have a written contract?   14

1.7 What is a deed and when is it necessary?   15

1.8 What's the effect of making a contract?   15

CHAPTER 2 Negotiating Contracts   **17**

2.1 What do I need to think about before I start negotiating?   19

2.2 What about strategy?   20

2.3 How do I keep track of the deal?   21

2.4 When and how should the draft contract be produced and reviewed?   23

2.5 When should I get professional help?   24

2.6 Why can't we start work now we've agreed all the basics?   25

2.7 What if the main terms are agreed but there is a fuller contract 'to follow'?   27

2.8 What if I make a mistake or the agreement is defective in some way?   27

CHAPTER 3 Written Contracts   **31**

3.1 Is there a typical contract structure and language?   33

3.2 An outline contract framework   33

3.3 The contract date   34

3.4 Details of the contract parties   35

3.5 Preliminary clauses   37

3.6 Defined terms   37

3.7 The main contract clauses   38

3.8 The final part of the contract   39

3.9 Aren't there different forms of contract layout too?   39

3.10 Some key words and phrases   40

CHAPTER 4 Selling Goods   **43**

4.1 How do I distinguish goods from services?   45

4.2 What about consumer sales – and implied terms?   45

4.3 What about the standard terms and conditions I often see?   46

4.4 Recording the detail   50

4.5 Title, retention of title, and risk   52

4.6 An example short form B2B Terms of Business   53

4.7 The sales chain and the different roles   56

4.8 How do I choose between distributor and agent?   57

4.9 What about exclusive arrangements?   59

4.10 What is different with sales to consumers?   60

CHAPTER 5 Supplying Services   **63**

5.1 How do you measure the quality of services?   65

5.2 How long do agreements for services last?   67

5.3 Do service providers have to be always available?   68

5.4 Price and payment   68

5.5 Independent contractor or employee? – The importance of the distinction   69

5.6 Confidentiality, intellectual property and restrictive covenants   71

5.7 Outsourcing   72

5.8 Transfer of employment – TUPE   73
5.9 A contract for services   75
5.10 Event planning scenario and examples   85

CHAPTER 6 Payment Terms   **93**
6.1 The contract price   95
6.2 What about price variations?   96
6.3 Payment date and credit periods   97
6.4 What about failure to pay?   98
6.5 Some contracts provide for royalties – how does that work?   99
6.6 Credit risk   100
6.7 Personal guarantees   101
6.8 Insolvency   102

CHAPTER 7 Innovation & Technology Issues   **105**
7.1 Managing the knowledge business   107
7.2 Intellectual property rights (IPR)   107
7.3 Can I protect an idea?   108
7.4 Non-disclosure agreements (NDAs)   109
7.5 Copyright   111
7.6 Other forms of IPR   114
7.7 Privacy and personal information   115
7.8 Technology contracts   116
7.9 Some examples   120

CHAPTER 8 Contracts & Risk   **123**
8.1 Introduction   125
8.2 Restricting the other party   126
8.3 Non-compete clauses (restrictive covenants)   127
8.4 Warranties and Indemnities   129
8.5 Exclusion and Limitation Clauses   131
8.6 Insurance   135
8.7 Competition Law   135

8.8 Negligence 137

8.9 The need for legal advice 137

CHAPTER 9 Living with Contracts **139**

9.1 Contracts as working documents 141

9.2 Transfer and assignment 142

9.3 'Boilerplate' clauses 144

9.4 Notices 144

9.5 Entire agreement 145

9.6 Force majeure 146

9.7 Choice of law and jurisdiction 147

9.8 Some other boilerplate clauses 148

9.9 Breach, Damages and Enforcement 149

CHAPTER 10 Ending Contracts **153**

10.1 How contracts end 155

10.2 How long should the term be? 156

10.3 How is a contract terminated when no one is in breach? 157

10.4 What about breach or insolvency? 159

10.5 What happens if one of the companies is taken over? 160

10.6 What if someone dies? 161

10.7 What happens after the contract ends? 162

10.8 What happens to employees on termination of a contract? 162

10.9 How do I best handle termination? 163

SUMMARY 10 Point Checklist **165**

Further reference **169**

Acknowledgements **171**

Index **173**

About the Author

AFTER QUALIFYING AS A SOLICITOR Charles joined a London City firm, rising quickly to partner. After a stint in a smaller practice, he started his own firm, which he ran and built up over several years before merging with another central London firm, becoming managing partner of the combined 35 partner practice some five years later. Having initially dealt with property matters he moved to company and commercial work, specialising for a period in employment law after ceasing his managing partner role, and then handled a broad range of merger and acquisitions work coupled with commercial contracts.

He has long had an affinity with developing businesses, acting for a range of family and other private companies in a variety of business fields. He devised and gave seminars on 'Law for Entrepreneurs' at Cranfield Management School and for many years ran updates on company and commercial law at a Cambridge college for those returning to the law. In 2004 he decided to go in-house with one of his major clients, The Random House Group Limited, where he built up and ran the legal function as Group Legal Director, recruiting and training his successor.

He has written *A Concise Business Guide to Contract Law* (1998) and *Business Contracts Handbook* (2010), both published by Gower/Ashgate. He holds a Cambridge MA and an MPhil in Critical Management from Lancaster University Management School.

Other activities include family, friends, walking, France, travel, wine, music and writing generally (including history and fiction).

Preface

WHILST MUCH OF BUSINESS is about preparation and application, it is the opportunities that are unplanned and from unexpected quarters that can give the greatest challenge. The origins of this book are in such a chance meeting. Having not long finished a lengthy book on business contracts (see Further Reference), I was not expecting to embark on another significant publishing project. Ultimately the temptation of distilling a complex subject into ten brief chapters aimed squarely at small businesses proved too strong, and this book is the result.

Small businesses, however, are as varied as the people who run them and the ideas they have, so there will be no typical reader. The challenge has been to give enough of a big picture to make the work approachable, along with examples and tips to make it informative and a useful business tool. If the result gives you an understanding of contracts and how to use them, and even more if it helps you with making better decisions for your business, it will have achieved its objective.

CHARLES BOUNDY
March 2012

Introduction

THIS BOOK IS SPECIFICALLY written for those running their own business. With so much else to think about, you might easily believe that contracts can wait. In fact the issues, like contracts themselves, will be there from the start; getting the best (or avoiding the worst) from contracts can be a major factor in how well and how quickly you succeed. So, whilst short and inevitably selective, this book aims to give you an overview of:

- how to make or avoid making a contract;

- what to include and what to look for in contracts;

- how to have the contract achieve what you want at the price you've agreed;

- how to identify and manage major contract risks;

- how to approach the negotiation of key issues;

- how to draft and manage the contract to best effect; and

- what to do (and not do) if things go wrong.

Some questions and myths

There are many misunderstandings about contracts, so here are eight common questions and myths.

1. I don't use contracts

In fact you make a contract every time you:

- go into a shop, select something to buy and pay for it;

- order something online;

- sign and return an order form (by post, email or online);

- order or lease a piece of office equipment;

- engage someone, including a freelancer, to help with your business;

- agree to provide or receive goods or services; or

- agree terms on a business deal.

2. Why are contracts important?

Each of these transactions creates a contract which governs exactly what is to be provided and what is to be received in return. If you don't provide what you have agreed, or you don't get what you were promised, there could be a breach of contract, possibly with serious results. Once the contract is made, its terms are fixed; afterwards, unless the other party agrees, there is no going back. So when you do create a contract you need to be sure you've got what you wanted for the price and on the terms you intended.

3. But don't contracts need to be in writing in some official form?

Although most business contracts are put in writing at some point (including letter and email), writing is not a legal requirement apart from a limited number of exceptions. So contracts can be, and often are, created informally, at a meeting or even in a phone conversation. What is always required is that there is a mutual intention to commit to a business deal. The real benefit of a written document is that it is clear evidence of exactly what was agreed at the time. Human memories being selective, and people being inclined to remember what they wanted to say rather than what they said, the best way to avoid a dispute about what was agreed is to have it written down and signed.

4. Why bother, as big companies insist on standard terms?

At times we're faced with standard terms and conditions, especially when using internet sites. This does not necessarily mean there are no alternatives, but if at the end of the day you feel you have no choice, you should know what you're signing up to. Unless you've been positively misled, you're deemed to have read and understood the terms you agree to in business, so you should know how those terms might affect you.

5. Even so, I can't afford to sue anyone, so what's the point?

Most cases don't come anywhere near court; even when they do, they hardly ever get to trial. That's partly because of the cost involved and largely because, once stripped back to the basics, the issue is either clear (such as with most non-payment cases) or there are arguments both ways, something the court process is designed to clarify. Once would-be litigants realise they might lose, they are more prepared to settle. In that negotiation, the stronger your supporting evidence, the better your likely settlement, and if the dispute does get serious, clear and thought-through contract terms should always give an advantage.

6. I'm not much good at writing things down and get confused by paperwork

You're not alone! Even if you don't want to get involved in the detail, this book can help you follow and use the key principles. You probably know someone who could help (never be too proud to ask someone you trust). If you are a visual person, try a mind-map or diagrams to help you through the process and choices. Ultimately to be successful you'll develop strengths that will give you clearer insights into key business decisions. Richard Branson, for example, turned dyslexia to his benefit, using his memory and business focus to best effect and recognising the skills of others in the areas where he felt himself less suited.

7. What about trading abroad?

This book primarily reflects English law. The laws of other countries (and individual states in the USA) may vary, so local advice is always recommended for international dealings, especially if problems arise.

Nevertheless, many of the principles here are of broad application; this applies both across the English-speaking world (the so-called 'common law' countries, including the USA, Canada, Australia, New Zealand and India, have English legal principles as founding influences on their laws) and with protocols such as the CISG (also known as the Vienna or UNCITRAL Convention). CISG is the UN Convention on Contracts for the International Sale of Goods, a uniform set of rules now adopted by more than 70 countries, but not the UK. If you operate or sell goods outside the UK you may need to become familiar with the CISG, but even here you'll find many of the principles explained in this book to be relevant.

Finally, both the use of English as the accepted common language of the Internet and the way English law adapts to and influences European law mean that the differences between laws in international trade are reducing all the time.

8. Don't I need a lawyer to help me with all this?

Using this book should help you understand most basic business contracts, assess what's important, ask the right questions and negotiate better. If you need a lawyer, it should save you time and money by knowing what to ask for and how to ask for it, and the book highlights issues where this is particularly recommended.

How much you can do yourself partly depends on the situation and partly what you are prepared to put into it. The chapters are, so far as possible, written in non-legal language, with technical terms explained and tips given throughout, with the aim of empowering you to handle contracts to the advantage of your business. And, as with any learning, practice makes all the difference.

Caveats

Especially with such limited space, this book is inevitably selective in concentrating on the major contract issues considered most likely to affect small businesses.

This book is therefore not a complete guide to business contracts and does not deal with specialist agreements, such as employment and finance contracts (and many others). For these reasons, because individual circumstances are always different, and also because the law continues to evolve, this book is not to be taken as legal advice as such nor as a substitute for professional help on your own situation, which is always recommended. Similarly, and for the same reasons, the various sample contracts are included as short-form illustrations and not as templates or precedents: accordingly no liability can be accepted for their use.

How to use this book

There are ten chapters. Each concentrates on a topic, cross-referencing where appropriate (marked # plus the chapter section), so that the overall picture emerges. After three chapters dealing with the basics of creating, negotiating and writing an effective contract, the remaining seven chapters go through the typical main contract provisions, concluding with the contract term and termination. This last chapter really is essential reading before you even start negotiating; it can be as important to know how to get out of something as how to get into it – and contracts are no exception!

The book can be read as a whole – or used as a guide. So, for example, a reader new to contracts or rusty on the basics should read chapters 1–3 and 10, and then go back to look at whichever of chapters 4–9 seem most relevant to their case. Those primarily selling goods should concentrate on chapters 4, 6 and 8, and those dealing in services chapter 5. Chapter 7 is likely to be very relevant to businesses involved in any element of creativity as well as technology. Chapters 8–10 will be a good starting point if you have problems with a current contract, cross-referencing back where appropriate.

CHAPTER 1
Contract Basics

1.1 What is a contract?

In practical terms, a contract is a legally binding agreement.

This requires:

- *actual agreement* on all the essential terms of the deal;
- sufficient *clarity and certainty* as to those terms;
- an *agreed price* or other exchange value (called 'consideration');
- the *intention to have a legal commitment*.

For the sake of simplicity it is generally assumed that there are only two parties to the transactions referred to in this book. The same principles nevertheless broadly apply to multi-party contracts.

1.2 What about the need for agreement?

Reaching agreement – Agreement is arrived at by one party making an offer to do something for the other on stated terms and the other accepting that offer. If the first offer is refused, that may be the end of the matter. If a *counter-offer* is made, such as a different price or other terms, that counter-offer cancels the original offer and creates a revised offer on the suggested new terms. That process can continue until the terms match.

- Stan Smith offers to sell Jenny Jones a computer system for her new business. He quotes a price, a delivery date and a fee for installation, commissioning and training.

- Jenny Jones thanks Smith for his offer, but says that whilst she would like to deal with him, she can get a better deal. That could be the end of the story.

- However, Jones goes on to say that she would buy from Smith if he reduced his price by 10% and included the additional costs within it. That is a counter-offer, open for Smith to accept or not. Note that if Smith refuses, Jones cannot go back to his original offer (unless Smith agrees), as this was cancelled by her counter offer.

- Smith might back away, but if he agrees Jones's proposal, that can create a contract. If, however, he throws in the extras and proposes a 5% discount rather than the 10% Jones requested, that is a further counter-offer, open for Jones to accept or refuse in turn.

- Unless and until Smith and Jones reach agreement, meaning that offer and acceptance match one another on all the essentials, there will be no contract.

What are the essential terms that have to be agreed? – These are the terms that give sufficient certainty to the contract, such as:

- what goods or services are to be supplied;

- by whom and to whom;

- what quantity or quality standards apply;

- what price (or exchange value) is to be paid or provided, and

- when and how this is to happen.

1.3 Clarity and certainty – what happens if everything is not clear?

The effect of lack of certainty – Let's take an agreement to buy goods; as a minimum a contract will need to specify the products, quantity and price. The delivery date may also be time-critical, but if the other terms are clear and certain, lack of an agreed date may not prevent a contract arising. In these cases the buyer is advised to specify the urgency and stipulate a date.

Implied terms – the principle

> If a key term is missing from a contract, the law will generally not imply what that term should be. If the basics are not agreed, there is probably no contract.

Exceptions to the principle – Here are four main exceptions:

- *terms implied by legislation* – legislation (e.g. the Sale of Goods Act) may imply some terms, such as that the goods are in satisfactory condition and fit for purpose (#4.2);

- *business efficacy* – where all the main terms are agreed and there is clear intent to have a binding agreement, the courts may imply a term where it is necessary to make the agreement work commercially;

- *previous dealings* between the same parties – where a 'course of dealings' on previously agreed terms is established between the parties (#4.3); and

- terms implied by *'custom and practice'* – a fall-back, but not to be relied on; each person's understanding of normal trade usage can differ, so if it's important to you it's best to set out clearly what is expected.

> It's best to have all the important terms sorted out and agreed at the outset. If some terms are implied, they may turn out not to be the terms you thought; they could be much worse!

1.4 I understand price but what is 'consideration'?

The need for value – Unless the agreement is in writing and signed as a deed (#1.7), there must always be value passing both ways in order to create a contract. This value element is what lawyers call *consideration*. So if Smith offers products to Jones, Jones must agree to pay for them in some valuable way in order for the commitment to be binding on Smith.

Price – Payment in money always satisfies the legal requirement for value. Payment may also be by exchange of goods or services which themselves have a value. Payment may even be nominal; provided there is some value. What is paid between businesses *does not have to be fair value*, as courts have no wish to get tied up in disputes over what is fair value in commercial trading. With sales to consumers (#4.2), however, the position is different and lack of overall fairness by the supplier may be heavily penalised.

1.5 Legal commitment

> The final key contract ingredient is that both parties intend to make a legal commitment.

Commitment – This is present in most business deals at the point when the parties have agreed all the essentials. It is like a legal handshake, the point when the deal is struck, also distinguishing the business deal from the friendly offer to help out. This commitment is the glue that confirms and holds the contract together.

Gentlemen's agreements – Not all business discussions are intended to lead to contracts. Conversations may be held and understandings reached which are no more than statements of hope or possible intention, never intended to be binding legal commitments. For a contract there has to be a genuine intention to be legally bound by *both* parties. Don't assume the other party is committed. If you're not sure, it's worth asking direct. If they're not committed, it is better to know, and if they are, they should not be offended by the inquiry. Likewise, if you don't want to be legally bound, make this explicit, especially before any work starts.

'To be agreed' / Agreements to agree – It is always tempting to leave a tricky issue until later, but leaving something 'to be agreed' or 'tba' is a red flag. There may be a settled intention to make a legal commitment, but unless the structure of the relationship is sufficiently spelled out, there may still be no contract. If the point is not agreed, it may be precisely because it's tricky, meaning greater risk of dispute about it later.

Don't leave things to be agreed later; you may find you haven't agreed the terms you thought or that you don't have a contract at all. If work has to start but it's really not practicable to agree all the detail up front, specify the essentials in an interim contract and set out what has still to be agreed plus how and by when it's to be agreed. This will give a court something to work with if there is a later dispute.

1.6 When do I need to have a written contract?

The advantage of written contracts – If all contract essentials are present, a legally binding agreement can arise without writing. But if there is a later dispute, memories tend to differ as to what was agreed, requiring events to be reconstructed (including phone calls, meetings and emails) to work out what might have been agreed and when. If the dispute goes to court, the judge will have to listen to witnesses and sift through all the documents to work out whether there is a contract and, if so, what its terms are, which can be a painful, expensive and uncertain process. Having the terms set out on paper and signed by both parties helps reduce the risk of that pain. Indeed, it's worth getting into the habit of putting things on paper (or email) from the start. If the other party is reluctant to do this you might reasonably wonder about *their* level of commitment.

> For most practical business purposes email suffices as writing and email headings or footers may be as good as a signature.

When a written document is necessary – The following cases are exceptions to the general principle:

- *Contracts relating to land* – need to be signed (for land transfers see #1.7 below);

- *Transfers of IP Rights* (such as copyright) – need to be in writing (but not agreements to transfer);

- *Personal or company guarantees* – need to be *evidenced* in writing;

- *Some consumer contracts* – (e.g. consumer finance and distance-selling agreements) have special rules;

- *Employment contracts* – need a written statement of terms just after employment starts;
- *Deeds* – some documents still require to be signed as a deed (#1.7).

1.7 What is a deed and when is it necessary?

When is a deed necessary? – It's wise to use a deed if there is any doubt as to whether there is consideration. On some occasions a deed is actually *necessary*. These include:

- Property (real estate) transfers (contracts to buy and sell property just need signing)
- Powers of attorney
- Some formal documents from other countries (which may require other formalities too)

The formalities of signing as a deed – All that is required (in England – other countries may vary) is:

- there is a *written document,*
- which specifies that it is to be '*signed as a deed*' by each party,
- whose signature is *witnessed* by an independent third party who also signs to that effect,
- with the document being *delivered* as a deed, which really means being handed over as such.

1.8 What's the effect of making a contract?

Commitment – A contract is a legal commitment. If you've forgotten something, or changed your mind, it's too late to change the contract, unless of course the other party also agrees. So you need to be certain before finalising the contract that you are able and committed to honour it.

> Once the contract is made, there's no going back. You are now entitled to require the other party to do what they've agreed to do and they are entitled to rely on you likewise.

The importance of timing – It follows then that you need to be conscious not just of what terms have been agreed but also *when and how* they are agreed. You may think you are still negotiating when in law a contract has already come into existence. Or you may think terms have been fixed when they haven't, which could lead you to deliver goods or undertake work for which you might not get paid. In the most serious cases, getting these things wrong could cripple a small business, as they do occasionally cripple big businesses. So you need to think about the negotiating process.

The longer-term relationship – The contract process is also an ideal opportunity to build a healthy relationship with a client or customer, working not only towards consensus in negotiation but also greater certainty in what is expected and how expectations can best be delivered. Winning new business is far more uncertain, time-consuming and costly than getting repeat orders, and whilst contracts will be the primary reference point if things go wrong, they are much more effective as tools to help get things right in the first place.

CHAPTER 2
Negotiating Contracts

2.1 What do I need to think about before I start negotiating?

Whether you expect heavy negotiations or to be dealing on standard terms it's worth planning at the start what you want (and don't want) from the contract. This can be done however works best for you; for example, if you like PowerPoint, this can be a good way of being focused and concise.

> Map out at the outset what you want and don't want from the deal.

Three key considerations to plan for:

1. The benefits – list all the benefits you expect to get out of the deal

- If you're selling goods or services, this may be money, in which case you'll want to know how much, when and where you'll get it and in what form.

- If you're buying goods or services you'll want to specify exactly what you expect, what it will achieve and when you'll get it.

2. The costs – what do you expect to do or pay for what you are getting (money or exchange value)?

- What's the basic cost of providing this?

- What else might you have to do or buy in?

- Are you dependent on anyone else and is there another contract you need in place first? If so, take care to link the two or make one contract subject to entering into the other by a given date.

- What about other related costs, such as insurance or on-going equipment maintenance?

- Have you fully factored in the impact of service taxes such as VAT?

3. The risks – what risks can you anticipate?

- What risks do you expect to take, and to what level? Could you resolve these or pay for them?

- Who should bear the other risks, and to what extent?

- If you are selling, what would happen if you didn't get paid? How could you mitigate that risk?

- If you are buying, what would happen if what you buy goes wrong or doesn't perform?

- What else might be likely to go wrong?

- How far can you/the other party get insurance against these risks and on what terms?

- Which risks or liability should be excluded or limited by the contract?

2.2 What about strategy?

Planning your strategy – You'll want to be sure you take the benefits of your negotiations through into the contract itself. Don't waste the negotiating effort with a lack of follow-through. Those who like the cut and thrust of negotiation don't always enjoy the contract process, but it can be best to draft at least the outlines as you negotiate.

Confidentiality – Before you start, consider whether you need to protect confidentiality, either of the negotiations themselves or because you'll be disclosing business information you'd rather keep secret. Look at #7.4 on this issue, and be careful who you tell and what you tell them.

> 'Subject to contract' – These are the magic words to avoid legal commitment before you are ready.

Subject to contract – Consider from the start writing: *'For the sake of clarity, our negotiations remain strictly subject to contract until a formal legal agreement has been agreed and signed by us both.'* Don't worry if you sound like a lawyer! But do then remember to make sure you get a signed agreement before starting work, as it will be hard to claim that the other party is committed if you've made everything subject to contract! Putting 'subject to contract' won't, however, unmake a contract that already exists, or where one party has already largely performed its 'duties', so the wording is not an infallible escape route. Note that 'without prejudice' means something entirely different. In practice you need only use that phrase if you are negotiating to resolve or avoid a dispute (#9.9).

> Planning your exit – Look at chapter 10 on ending contracts at this stage. Knowing how to exit at the right time and in the right way can be as important as getting into the contract in the first place.

2.3 How do I keep track of the deal?

The rolling deal memorandum – One way to combine negotiation and the contract processes is to build up the key issues by stages in the form of a rolling memo. This helps keep the original objectives (benefits) firmly in focus, with the costs and risks monitored as you go along. The memo can then be a good basis for drafting the contract or briefing a lawyer, saving much time, effort and cost in the process.

Meetings, phone calls and emails – Negotiations are typically conducted by a mix of emails and/or phone calls with occasional meetings.

- *Meetings* – Meetings help build relationships and trust and can be best for resolving detail or problems. Even then, it's sensible to follow meetings with a written note of what was agreed – or not agreed – and to update the rolling memorandum. Remember that if you agree everything at a meeting and agree to go ahead, that might create a binding contract there and then, so make it clear at the outset that everything is subject to contract – if that is still the intention.

- *Phone calls* – Contracts can also be made over the phone, so take care with the language used.

- *Emails* – As emails can create or evidence a contract, avoid making commitments until you are ready.

> Email is immediate and provides a written record, so take great care when using it, especially if any emotion is involved. On the other hand, if you are fully aware of the situation and want to secure a commitment, you may be able to agree a contract by email.

Reaching agreement – As we've seen, there may be a series of offers and counter-offers, probably covering the headline terms only, and possibly anticipating that if agreement is reached, a fuller document will follow. Sooner or later the time will come when one party will go no further and the other has to decide either to accept or walk away. If there is agreement, and assuming this remains subject to contract as above, the process of negotiating the written contract will start, if it hasn't already done so.

> The big risks here are having the whole project delayed by a slow contract negotiation or becoming impatient (or optimistic) and starting work before everything has been finalised and signed off.

2.4 When and how should the draft contract be produced and reviewed?

The objective – A written contract records and clarifies the bargain that the parties have agreed in principle. Contract negotiation is ideally a key phase in developing the business relationship, rather than a form of gladiatorial contest. Whether you are preparing the contract or reviewing someone else's draft, it's best to be clear at the start what you want and to hold out for that; you can then perhaps be pragmatic on other issues of lesser concern.

The draft contract – Chapter 3 deals with the framework and language of contracts. A key issue here is *expectation management*, so that the first draft contract reflects the detail and spirit of what has been agreed, indicates any unresolved issues (through square brackets for example) and does not contain major surprises. This can help avoid the familiar howls of anguish that typically result from sight of the first draft. Even so, some anguish is probably inevitable, because human beings are often challenged by seeing (or avoiding!) their intentions as commitments in black and white print! Here are some ways the process might be better managed:

- Start work on the contract early. If you're trying to save on legal costs, don't wait too long.

- Prepare a rolling or deal memo in the meantime and keep it updated. It will save you time and money.

- Consider sharing the deal memo with the other party to ensure mutual understanding.

- Consider how the other party is likely to react and prepare the ground appropriately.

> Brief whoever drafts the contract so they understand and reflect the deal spirit and key issues.

2.5 When should I get professional help?

Using lawyers – There is plenty you can do; there will also be times when you need to concentrate on what you do best and when it's better to use a lawyer. It's easy to be cynical about lawyers, but they are human beings, most of whom prefer an involvement with what you do and are keen to do a good job for you; many are also experienced negotiators. Some suggestions as to working with them follow.

> Generally, remember that lawyers are cautious by professional training, so be as specific as possible as to what you do and don't want; otherwise they'll be inclined to give you more than you need.

- *Invest some time* – When you first deal with lawyers, take time to get to know them and explain your business. This helps them spot key issues and avoid spending time on the wrong things. They will often not charge for a first meeting if they think the relationship will develop.

- *Give clear instructions* – Don't ask them: 'Could you just have a look at this for me and check it's OK?' You might get a ten-page letter back at considerable cost. Tell them what you want to know and how, or ask them to look through the agreement and then book a call or meeting to discuss it. Use the rolling memorandum as a brief. Remember that lawyers mostly charge by time, so help them to use their time well. By the same token, however, don't expect them necessarily to alert you to an issue you did not ask about!

- *Be realistic* – Be clear about benefit, cost and risk. Without understanding how you see these fundamentals lawyers have little chance of producing or negotiating the right contract for you. Above all, be clear where and to what extent you'll accept some risk. Without this they'll try to produce a risk-free contract, which, even if it existed, would be impossible to negotiate or actually enforce.

- *Concentrate on probabilities rather than remote possibilities* – You can never cover every possibility, so concentrate on things that experience tells you are more likely rather than trying to cover remote risks.

- *Insist on relevance* – If your lawyer drafts the contract, request something short, relevant and balanced; it's normally better to have something you can understand, operate, agree, get signed quickly and be able to work with than an all-singing, all-dancing but ultimately impractical document.

Other advisers – You may need other advisers, such as accountants or tax specialists on what form of business vehicle to have or the potential effects of service taxes/VAT, withholding taxes, capital allowances, loss reliefs or other tax issues.

2.6 Why can't we start work now we've agreed all the basics?

Jumping the gun – Once key terms seem agreed, the air is full of possibility and goodwill and there may be impatience to get started. A written contract may not seem important or may be expected to take too long. The first is not true and the second need not be. All too often work is started before everything is agreed and signed.

Sometimes showing willing and pressing on bring its rewards, but experience shows that jumping the gun in this way may lead to uncertainty and grief when expectations ultimately don't match or aren't realised. How to avoid this?

> One way, if there is real pressure to start work early, is to have a short binding contract for the preliminary stages only, making it clear that negotiations for other terms and a fuller contract will continue on a 'subject to contract' basis in the meantime.

- *Take one step at a time* – Avoid promising anything longer-term until everything is agreed. The fact that either of you could walk away after the initial stages helps keep you both on your toes in the meantime, but you then need to be prepared for the fact there may be no stage two.

- *Stipulate any conditions* – for achievement of the preliminary stages or approving the quality of the work done, raising any issues quickly and clearly.

- *Specify payment and payment dates* – Try to agree a day rate or stage payments for the initial stages.

- *IP rights* – Specify who owns any intellectual property rights in anything new being created, concentrating on the preliminary stages only (see chapter 7.)

- *Allocate risks* – Assess any material risks and specify who bears them and to what extent (see chapter 8.)

- *Restrictions* – Limit exclusivity discussions or other restrictions to what is essential to the preliminary work (#8.2) and think whether it may be better to see how the relationship works before committing further.

- *Keep it simple* – Use a more basic form of agreement unless the full length 'standard' contract really is suitable.

2.7 What if the main terms are agreed but there is a fuller contract 'to follow'?

It's not uncommon for the principals to hammer out a deal and perhaps exchange emails or agree (and even sign) a *letter of intent* (LOI) with the comment that a fuller form of agreement will follow later, perhaps once drafted by the lawyers.

This can be useful in enabling progress to be made but could become problematic and lead to disputes if the fuller agreement never materialises or, if it does, is not agreed and signed. Unless the emails or LOI make this clear, there will be uncertainty as to whether or not there is already a binding contract. If the 'agreement' is provisional, the emails or LOI should make it clear that the deal remains 'subject to contract'. The words 'subject to board approval', for example, do not have the same effect. If there is intended to be a binding agreement, the emails or LOI should state this and that the fuller contract will deal with the detail.

2.8 What if I make a mistake or the agreement is defective in some way?

The principles – You are taken to have read and understood the contract (whether you've done so or not!), so if you just make a mistake or a bad bargain, you'll probably have to suffer the consequences. If, however, you have been misled or deceived in some way, or if there was something seriously wrong with how the contract was negotiated, you may have legal rights to damages or even to set the contract aside.

Mistake as to the identity of the other party – Check you know who you are dealing with. The law is unlikely to help if you just assume the other party is better off or more able than they actually are, but it may act if the other person's identity is critical to the deal and you have been deliberately deceived about it.

Mistake as to what the contract is about – if you are deceived into signing a totally different type of document (say, a mortgage on your house rather than a new desk order), the law may help.

Mistake as to the content of the contract – If you can prove (e.g. by earlier email exchanges that had not been re-negotiated later) that the final contract did not reflect the terms you had actually agreed, *rectification* may be available. This means changing the contract to reflect properly what had been agreed, but is something of a last-ditch approach, normally only available if you can show that *both* parties genuinely made a mistake or that *one* party *unfairly* relied on a mistake made by the other (such as by noticing it but not pointing it out).

Misrepresentation – The old stories of used car salesmen making outrageous claims for the cars they are selling are less common now, but in any contract negotiation one or even both parties may make statements designed to encourage the other to agree a deal or pay more for something than they would otherwise have done. These statements can be *representations*, and if they turn out to be false (and are more than just casual sales talk), they may amount to *misrepresentations*, entitling the buyer to claim damages (based on the reduced value of what was actually bought) or in extreme cases to cancel (*rescind*) the whole contract and get the purchase price back.

> The misrepresentation might not have been dishonest; false representations even made innocently may be enough to set the contract aside if major and the victim actually relied on them.

Actual and apparent authority – When dealing with companies check that the company has indeed been duly formed and registered and that the person you are dealing with is authorised to agree and sign the contract. Job titles like 'director' and 'manager' effectively hold out these officials as having authority to enter into contracts, whatever the internal sign-off rules may be, giving those with senior job titles *ostensible authority* to agree contracts. But at lower levels it's sensible to get a more senior manager to sign so as to reduce the risk of the company otherwise disclaiming the contract.

Dealing with children – Apart from the so-called 'necessaries' of life (essential food, clothing, housing, medicine and the like), if you sell something to someone under 18 (in England; 16 in Scotland) they can technically get their money back if (and it may be a big 'if') they return the goods. In practice it is usually best to have a child's parents or guardian sign any agreement with the child, and then have the 'child' adopt (formally accept) the contract on reaching the age of 18.

Illegality – The courts will not enforce illegal provisions in contracts and may refuse to enforce the clause in question or even the agreement overall if the illegal term is key to the contract. The same may apply if the contract is contrary to public policy, such as an unregulated gaming contract. Illegality could mean that you'd be unable to recover payment due to you under the contract, so it is something to watch out for.

CHAPTER 3
Written Contracts

3.1 Is there a typical contract structure and language?

Contract structure – Contracts can come in all shapes and sizes, but need a framework, like a container holding the contents together. This chapter is about the container and later chapters investigate the contents.

The language of contracts – As can be seen from the examples in this book, contracts need clear wording but don't need complex language. Undue complexity can create confusion, which can breed uncertainty and dispute. If you are drafting, keep it simple, use short sentences, and build up the clauses as you go along.

> If the contract meaning is disputed, the judge will need to decide what the parties must have intended it to mean at the time they made it, giving words their ordinary meaning unless the context indicates otherwise. So if you or the other party don't understand it, or an intelligent bystander couldn't follow it, you could have a problem!

Punctuation – Contracts can use and benefit from punctuation, if and when used correctly.

3.2 An outline contract framework

The following is a useful starting framework for most cases:

1. The date of the agreement
2. The parties to the agreement
3. Any preliminary clauses

4. Any defined terms

5. The main contract clauses

6. Schedules/appendices and signature provisions.

Conventions used – Italics are used in the text of this book for emphasis or to highlight new legal expressions. Sample clauses use the following conventions (which are not necessarily of general application).

- **BOLD CAPITALS** = document title, schedule headings and signature headers;

- **Bold type** – lower case = the first time a term is defined;

- [Text in square brackets] = alternative text;

- *Italics (**bold** and unbold)* = instructions as to actual names / details to be filled in according to circumstances.

3.3 The contract date

Contracts can just start with the date of the agreement. This doesn't need fancy language if it's clear that there is an agreement, but the date is important. For example:

[PRODUCTION] **AGREEMENT**

Date [*or* **Agreement dated**] [*add date when contract signed*]

- *Don't pre-date or post-date a contract* – The date should be the date the contract is signed by all parties; pre-dating or post-dating a contract could lead to problems. For example, the contract date may be highly significant for some tax purposes, and should not be misleading. If the date has already been incorrectly pre-dated on the contract you're asked to sign, delete it, write in the correct date and initial the change.

- *Linkage* – Take care if the contract date is linked to a particular contract clause, e.g. the term starts from the contract date. Changing the contract date might have unexpected effects if work has already started or is not due to start for some time. (See also the example in #10.1.)

- *Signing subject to a condition* – Some signed contracts are left on hold (in escrow in legal parlance) until a pre-agreed event or fulfilment of a stated condition. The contract may not be intended to become fully 'live' until that event has occurred or the condition has been fulfilled. So you need first to agree and record what the event or condition is, and second whether both parties are bound to wait to see if the event or condition happens or is fulfilled or whether they can still pull out before it occurs. There should also be an agreed latest date for the escrow condition to be fulfilled.

3.4 Details of the contract parties

The names of the parties should be correctly set out. With individuals, full names are advisable but not normally essential provided there is no dispute as to who each person actually is; adding a home address also helps. With *limited liability enterprises* (a company or a limited liability partnership – LLP) the correct name can be very important (see below). Defining the parties at the outset is also useful, although practice varies greatly. This book uses *Supplier* and *Customer* in the examples for convenience because the names apply for goods or services. Defining one party as '*the Company*' can be confusing if both are limited companies!

PARTIES:

(1) [**Full personal or registered company name**] [(registered in [England] with number *[company number if registered])* of [*or* whose registered office is at *[address]*] (**Supplier**); and

(2) [**Full personal or correct registered company name**] **Limited** (registered in [England] with number [*company number if registered*]) [of [*or* whose registered office is at] [*address*]] (**Customer**).

Or as this might appear in a final contract:

PARTIES

(1) **Toy Balloon Limited** (registered in England with number 123456) of 99 Inflation Way, Portsmouth, PO21 2UG (**Supplier**); and

(2) **Party First Limited** (registered in England with number 987654) of 5 Jubilation Gardens, Midhurst, W. Sussex, GU67 8IL (**Customer**).

Company names – Company names should exactly match their name as recorded at Companies House (or its equivalent elsewhere). If you can't find the name, there may be a mistake somewhere, you may be dealing with an overseas company (many have the suffix 'limited') or something could be more amiss. The wrong company name may not be the one you thought you were dealing with, or may be no company at all. And company names can be (and often are) changed quite legitimately. A company search will show this. The only thing that does not change is the registered company number. So it's wise to do a search at the Companies Registry (or its equivalent) to check the name and company number of the company you're dealing with against any stationery you have seen. For a small fee company registration agents will do some fuller searching for you.

Don't sign for the wrong company. Those signing contracts are deemed by law to warrant they have authority to sign. If the company doesn't exist, they are in breach of warranty and may be personally liable to honour the company's obligations.

3.5 Preliminary clauses

Preliminary clauses, sometimes headed 'whereas', can be useful in explaining (or *reciting*) relevant background to the contract. Thus they are traditionally called 'recitals'. They can also help clarify the intention of the parties and may be useful if disputes arise later about clause meanings. The following is a very basic example:

> **BACKGROUND** [*or* **PRELIMINARY**]
>
> (A) Supplier provides [*description of goods*]
>
> (B) [Following previous dealings] Customer has requested and Supplier has agreed to provide goods for the price and on the terms set out in this agreement.

3.6 Defined terms

The principles – Defined terms are valuable to clarify the meaning of words or phrases used several times in a contract, and to avoid repetition. Here are some tips as to how to use them to best effect:

- Once defined, use them in the text with an initial capital letter, and keep checking the definition.

- If they are used to clarify supposedly understood industry phrases or acronyms, make sure they are clear and agreed, as such things often mean different things to different people.

- Remember to apply them consistently, watching the effect any changes to the definitions may have on the contract obligations and vice versa.

- Check they are not 'circular', meaning that definitions don't just cross-refer to one another without pinning down what the terms mean.

A basic approach – If the contract is straightforward with few defined terms, you might put definitions in the recitals or text as you go along, in quotation marks or highlighted in bold, as this example shows.

> Supplier has agreed to sell and Customer has agreed to buy *[number] [product description]* (**Products**) for the sum of *[purchase price expressed in appropriate currency]* [each] plus VAT (or other equivalent sales tax) (**Price**) for delivery at Supplier's expense at Customer's UK premises at *[specify address]* (**Delivery**) no later than *[date]* (**Latest Delivery Date**)

An alternative approach – Often definitions are set out in their own section or clause, either at the start of the contract or in a schedule at the back if they are lengthy.

3.7 The main contract clauses

After the names of the parties and the preliminary clauses the contract is likely to cover the following:

- *Operative clauses* – setting out the parties' actual performance obligations (#4 and 5);

- *Financial terms* – setting out the payment terms in detail (#6);

- *Managing innovation and technology* – dealing with confidentiality, copyright (and other rights in *intangible* or *intellectual property*) and relevant technology issues (#7);

- *Contracts and risk* – clauses managing risk (restrictions, warranties, indemnities and liability limitation (#8));

- *Living with contracts* – the 'small print' sections including typical 'boilerplate' clauses (#9); and

- *Term and termination clauses* – covering how long the contract lasts and how it can be brought to an end, either on a no-fault basis or following breach or insolvency, and what happens afterwards (#10).

3.8 The final part of the contract

Schedules or appendices – These (usage varies as to which word is used) are integral parts of the contract, normally separate sections at the end for ease of reference. Whilst schedules should not be used as operative clauses, they can be useful means of setting out product specifications, key performance indicators (KPIs) or complex royalty calculations.

Signature provisions – Many contracts finish with the signature provisions, after the main clauses and either before or after any schedules or appendices. In either case, what matters is that the correct names of the parties are used and that all parties to the contract (or those authorised by them) sign. The signature of an individual party or a director on behalf of a corporate party is all that is required, except for deeds, which require a witness to each signature.

3.9 Aren't there different forms of contract layout too?

Certainly – Provided the four essentials in #1.1 are present, the contract form can vary greatly. Many contracts are in letter form, such as the example at #5.9. A heads of terms (HoT) or letter of intent (LOI) formula may also be used, dealing with the issues in much the same way as a more formal agreement. Each form will, however, ideally address all the issues mentioned in #3.7 and described further in these chapters.

Attaching terms and conditions – Many business contracts have a pro forma front page with sections or boxes to be filled in detailing the parties, the goods or services being supplied, the price and perhaps the term of the contract. That will probably be the signature page too. The rest of the terms are on the reverse or on an attached set of terms and conditions which are included (or incorporated) into the contract by a clause to that effect on the front sheet.

> Terms and conditions may look just like small print but they can contain some important provisions that might affect you, including hidden traps such as a rolling term, price escalation and limited termination rights. So they need as much attention as if set out in a full contract.

3.10 Some key words and phrases

Finally here it's worth considering a few legal phrases that regularly appear in contracts.

Good faith – Courts in England and other common law countries now recognise obligations of good faith on contract parties. One judge summarised the duty of both parties to act in good faith as '*genuinely to do their best to achieve [an agreed] desired result and not merely to go through the motions*'. It also involves a fair degree of honesty; for example one party might not act in good faith if it fails to notify the other of a significant change in circumstances that could impact the contract performance. Even so, good faith obligations need a health warning. An obligation to '*negotiate in good faith'* to agree something in the future requires honesty, but probably doesn't prevent each party having regard to its own commercial interests to get the best deal for itself! Once, however, joint objectives are agreed and sufficiently crystallised, the obligation to use good faith to achieve those objectives is likely to be enforceable.

Reasonable / reasonable notice / unreasonably withheld – English judges, on the other hand, have had centuries of practice in deciding what is '*reasonable*', what a reasonable man would do in the circumstances or what would be unreasonable refusal of consent. As ever, being more specific is the best way to limit misunderstanding and potential costly dispute.

Reasonable / best endeavours – The strongest obligation on a party is actually *to do* or *not to do* something. Where an absolute commitment is impractical, or can't be agreed, the obligation may be limited to *endeavours* (or in US contracts *endeavors* or *efforts*). The precise interpretation of an endeavours obligation will depend on the circumstances.

A **best endeavours** obligation, whilst not normally requiring the party to take unreasonable steps, is still extremely strong; unless you are prepared for a potentially very high degree of effort (and possible high cost), you'd be better to limit your obligations to **reasonable endeavours**. Even better, when possible, is to minimise the risk of dispute by setting out the actual steps required to fulfil the obligation and to state whether or not the party in question can take its own commercial interests into account.

For the avoidance of doubt – Here's a phrase that sometimes creates doubt where there was none before! It is best used sparingly – if at all – with better efforts made to draft the clause or obligation more precisely.

Including but not limited to – We love to list things, and this phrase is used to avoid the application of the legal principle that if you list things, your list is deemed to cover everything of the kind you are referring to. (See for example para. 6 of the sample letter in #5.9.)

Jointly and severally – When contracting with two or more parties – companies or individuals – consider making their obligations *joint and several*. This means that *each of them* (severally) is liable for all their *joint obligations* (and breaches). It helps to ensure that if there is a problem they work together with you to find a solution, whatever the rights and wrongs between them personally.

Condition – A condition is something that has to be done or fulfilled, often as requirement for something else. *Condition precedent* indicates that the requirement must be fulfilled before the contract becomes fully effective (such as consent from a third party). Use the term carefully; breach of or failure to fulfil a condition may be seen as a *material breach* (#10.4).

Representation – A representation is a statement of fact or capability, for example what a person or a product can actually do (see #2.8). The term again should be used carefully since a false representation, even made innocently, can trigger not just a damages claim but also, in extreme cases, the right to terminate the contract.

Warranties – This is a similar form of statement of fact, often used in conjunction with representation; breach of warranty can give rise to damages for the actual loss caused, but normally won't justify termination unless the warranty is fundamental to the contract.

Indemnity – This is an obligation to pay money to make good a third party claim ('hold harmless'). Some indemnities are drafted very widely, pushing major elements of risk onto the indemnifying party, so they need checking and can be the subject of extensive negotiation (see #8.4 on negotiating warranties and indemnities).

CHAPTER 4
Selling Goods

4.1 How do I distinguish goods from services?

Goods, services or both? – Most business contracts involve selling goods or providing services of some kind. Obviously goods are generally physical and services non-physical (or *intangible*), but this distinction is becoming more problematic. Take two examples:

- *Digital entertainment products* – Here content is held digitally and the product may be available either in physical form (such as CD or DVD) or downloaded from an internet supplier. Both ultimately give the consumer access to the same content, but CDs/DVDs are technically goods and downloads are services. Sometimes there may be different sales tax/VAT treatment, as with books in the UK, zero-rated in physical form but charged at standard rate as eBooks. This may in turn affect your need to register for VAT.

- *Computer programs* – These are essentially intangible, consisting of binary code designed for a specific purpose, incorporated into a physical product, such as a computer or a disk, or increasingly downloaded in pure digital form.

So, particularly in legislating for fair treatment for consumers, lawmakers have been moving to laws that govern the sale of both physical and intangible 'products' generically.

4.2 What about consumer sales – and implied terms?

Consumer sales – Another distinction is between *business to business sales (B2B)* and *business to consumer sales (B2C – or D2C if the sale is from producer 'direct to consumer')*. The definition of *consumer* varies slightly between regulations but generally means the *'end user'* or person who actually enjoys (or consumes) the relevant product (or service). Consumer sales tend to be heavily regulated and consumers increasingly protected by law. With ready export markets, the chance of offending some other country's laws with sales to consumers there can be high. So even if you are not selling D2C, you should consider potential exposure to product liability and consumer protection laws where the ultimate consumer is based, both directly and indirectly through your contracts with resellers selling into those markets.

Implied terms – As mentioned in #1.3 some legislation, such as the updated *Sale of Goods Act (SGA)* and associated statutes, and the *Supply of Goods and Services Act* (affecting services or supply such as hiring and leasing agreements), will imply terms into contracts. Some of these implied terms can be overridden by the contract, but others cannot, especially with consumer sales. Some examples of implied terms:

- *Title* – the seller must own the goods at the time of sale

- *Quality* – the goods must be of satisfactory quality

- *Description* – the goods must comply with the description or sample given

- *Marketing* – advertising and marketing of the goods must not mislead consumers

- *Exclusions* – any exclusion or limitation of liability for defects must be reasonable.

4.3 What about the standard terms and conditions I often see?

How it works legally – When companies insist on their own 'standard' *terms and conditions of business (TOB)*:

- If the seller sells by catalogue or the web, the products will be as shown in the catalogue or web page.

- The customer selects and confirms the order by post, phone or through website acceptance and payment.

- The TOB, set out in the catalogue or referred to on the website, will apply provided clearly referred to and reasonably accessible (sometimes by separate web-link), whether actually read or not.

Buyer's TOB – Many large businesses also have their own terms which they seek to use when *buying* goods. This can lead to conflict (see battle of the forms below).

Why does it matter whose terms apply? – TOB will often cover issues such as delivery and payment, short or late delivery, defective goods, late payment or insolvency of one of the parties, events which, sadly, occur all too often in business.

Drafting standard terms of business – Some standard terms, when closely inspected, turn out to be muddled or inconsistent with the way the business actually works. Often this is because they have been 'borrowed' from another company or have been tinkered with by different people and never properly stitched together. So it's worth getting the right terms for *your* business – and keeping them updated.

Negotiating standard terms – Weigh up at the outset what material costs or risks are likely to be involved and how far what you are buying is critical for your business. Is there a choice of another supplier or customer? You may just accept the position if you want the products, but you might try the following:

- Go through the TOB to see what problems arise, and ask the seller to change any that seem oppressive, unfair or disproportionate; ask to go up the management chain if necessary;

- If changes are agreed, try to get these in writing in the contract or, if that's not possible, put them in writing to the seller as agreed points *before* the contract is signed or accepted; that may at least give you some legal arguments if things go wrong;

- If the seller is obdurate and won't change anything, you could write stating the points, saying you've asked to change them and that the seller has refused; if the issue ever becomes litigious that might just help you under the Unfair Contract Terms Act (#8.5).

> Act in a measured way and state why the offending terms are inappropriate; even big businesses may be reluctant to appear completely unreasonable.

Incorporating terms and conditions into the contract – To be legally effective a term has to be included *before* the contract comes into existence. This is called *incorporating* the term into the contract, and if it is not properly incorporated it won't apply. So concluding the contract and sending terms *afterwards* generally won't work. *Sellers* normally deal with this issue by:

- using an order form expressly stating that orders are subject to TOB; *and*

- ensuring the TOB are a) set out on the reverse of the order form, or b) sent through to the customer before the order is confirmed, or c) referred to on a readily accessible website or other location.

Just stating 'terms and conditions available on request' (if indeed they are) may work, but is less reliable.

Course of dealing – If TOB are just sent on the back of an invoice, this will generally be ineffective, since the contract will already have been made, unless the seller can show a *course of dealing* between the same parties such that, even if the terms did not apply to the first sale, the buyer was on notice of and deemed to accept them before subsequent sales.

The battle of the forms – What if both seller and buyer have their own standard terms? You'd then have to go through the sequence of events to find out when the contract was concluded. Each counter-offer destroys the original offer and sets up a new offer which is in turn capable of acceptance. So if the seller offers to sell on its terms, the buyer accepts but insists on its own terms and the seller then supplies, the seller may be deemed to have accepted the buyer's counter-offer and the buyer's terms will probably apply. But if the court decides that neither would ever have agreed to the other's terms, but there is still a contract, neither party's terms might apply, leaving default provisions to apply, for example the implied terms of the Sale of Goods Act (#4.2.)

Sample short-form Supply of Products clause – This wording assumes that Products is a defined term and the supplier has TOB dealing with much of the detail (#4.5). As the contract will prevail over the TOB (see b) below) the buyer should seek to introduce into the contract at this point any protection it feels necessary, including seeking to amend the reference to complying with all applicable laws (#4.2).

a) Supplier will on or within [seven] days before *[date]* supply and deliver the Products to Customer's premises at *[details of delivery address]* [and/or any other address in [England] within [50 miles] of that address as nominated in writing by Customer to Supplier at least 14 days before the relevant delivery] in good and satisfactory condition, in accordance with [all applicable laws and regulations and] the terms of this agreement.

b) [Supplier's terms and conditions of supply *(last revised date)* will apply to the supply of all Products by Supplier to Customer as if set out in full in this agreement. The terms of this agreement will prevail if there is any inconsistency between it and Supplier's terms and conditions of supply.]

4.4 Recording the detail

Description – First, state clearly what products are being supplied in a way that both parties can follow; just quoting the supplier's catalogue number may be meaningless to the buyer.

> A useful test – would a sensible third party seeing or overhearing the deal terms understand what was being sold, and whether what was delivered conformed to what was ordered?

Number or quantity – Define how many products are being ordered or how else the quantity is to be measured, such as weight or volume. When the sale is by reference to weight or volume, consider whether there may be some acceptable margin of under- or over-delivery, and the effect on price.

Delivery – Some key points to cover here are:

- *Date* – What is the (earliest and) latest date for delivery?

- *Location and cost* – Where are the goods to be delivered and at whose cost?

- *Proof of delivery (POD)* – Must there be a signed and dated POD to minimise later disputes? (But beware hidden statements in PODs confirming that goods are in good condition if they've not been inspected.)

- *Deemed delivery* – Some contracts (such as 'ex-works' delivery) specify delivery as the point when the goods leave (or are even available for collection from) the supplier's factory or warehouse, in which case buyer and not supplier becomes responsible for the transport operation and risks.

Export – Are there any export considerations involved? Planning, cost and risk increase considerably with transport across national borders. This is a specialised area, and the parties may benefit from referring to international standards, such as *Incoterms*, to ensure their understanding is the same.

Timing issues and time of the essence – Suppliers are often reluctant to commit to delivery dates; even where they do, failure to deliver on time may not be regarded as a material breach, or may be able to be remedied (as to 'material breach' see #10.4).

> If there are special products (like perishable food) or time of delivery is critical for some other reason (such as a new store opening, a new IT project or onward sale) consider making time of the essence so far as delivery is concerned. The recitals might explain the importance of such events.

This can be done by adding a provision to the contract – or sending a formal notice after the original date has been missed – specifying a reasonable latest date for delivery or completion and stating that 'time is of the essence' in respect of the revised delivery date. This will mean that if the due date (or revised fair date) is missed, the buyer can then cancel the contract and claim from the supplier for loss caused by the delay. This may be hard to negotiate but should be reviewed against the risk to your business if delivery is late.

Quality issues – The legal implication that goods must be of 'satisfactory' quality is not precisely defined, so ideally buyers should:

- have the contract or specification set out any specific quality standards;

- inspect goods as soon as practicable after delivery;

- promptly notify in writing any potential defects as a record, as per the notices clause (#9.4); and

- reject promptly and unambiguously any goods that are seriously defective (e.g. by returning them with a clear rejection statement) since the right to reject goods can be lost very quickly.

Sellers should require buyers to inspect the goods and notify any apparent defects as soon as practicable; if the goods are pre-packed for resale, the TOB should allow a sensible period for the inspection.

4.5 Title, retention of title, and risk

Title means the legal ownership of goods and *risk* in goods is liability for loss or damage to them. Risk and title pass on delivery unless the contract states otherwise. To give the seller some security most TOB delay title passing until the goods have been paid for, which may well be 30 or 60 days later. This is known as *retention of title* (ROT), giving an unpaid seller the right to recover its goods if the buyer fails to pay for them. In practice this right will normally only be exercised if the buyer becomes insolvent, when the claim against the buyer will be handled (and scrutinised for any weakness) by the qualified insolvency practitioner (#6.8) acting on the insolvency.

ROT clauses should be clear whether title is retained until *those goods* have been paid for or until *all* goods sold by that supplier to that buyer have been paid for (an '*all monies due*' clause). The clause should also specify that the buyer must keep the goods separate and permit the seller to have access to them to exercise its rights, although if goods are resold in the normal course of business before insolvency, title will usually pass to the sub-buyer at that point. If this area is significant to your business, early legal advice is recommended.

Risk – Again, the contract should clarify when risk passes from supplier to buyer, and each party should check that its insurance cover ties in with when risk passes under the contract terms.

Storage and handling – Many suppliers operate via a distributor or aggregator which, either taking title to the goods or handling them as agent, receives, stores and then delivers them according to customer orders. Service quality issues, covered in chapter 5, may be relevant here. Again, the contract terms need to be closely considered to check who bears the risk of loss or damage of goods after receipt, and may include limitation of liability clauses (#8.5).

4.6 An example short form B2B Terms of Business

These principles can be seen at work in the following example. The terms are drafted to go on the back of an order form, which will define Supplier (seller), Customer (buyer), Products, Price, delivery address, Payment Date and Designated Bank Account. Underlined text shows potential Buyer/Customer changes to make the arrangement more mutual. The customer may also want to challenge the sole remedy provision in 7 (see #8.5). Note that the right to cancel in 2b. is a softer alternative to making time of the essence, possibly more palatable to the Supplier. (Note that these are not suitable for sales to consumers.)

Short-form Terms of Business (for Business to Business Sales)

1. **Applicability** – These terms and conditions (**Terms**) apply to each order for Products (**Order**) made by Customer and accepted by Supplier on the order form overleaf (**Order Form**).

2. **Delivery.**

a. Supplier will deliver Products to Customer at the delivery address shown in the Order Form (**Delivery**). Delivery takes place when Products are delivered to Customer's premises.

b. Supplier will deliver as soon as reasonably practicable but does not guarantee any delivery date and will have no liability to Customer for any delay in delivery [, except that if Supplier is unable to complete Delivery within 14 days after the estimated delivery date Customer may by written notice to Supplier cancel the Order with no liability attaching to either party];

c. Customer has no right to return Products or to a refund except for damaged Products strictly as set out below.

3. **Price and payment.**

Customer will pay the Price (shown on the Order Form) plus VAT at the applicable rate in cleared funds to Supplier's Designated Bank Account on or before the Payment Date.

4. **Risk in Products.**

Risk in the Products will pass to Customer immediately on Delivery.

5. **Title to Products.**

Title to Products will remain with Supplier until all amounts due to Supplier from Customer for the Products [and on any other account between Supplier and Customer] have been paid in full [or until earlier resale by Customer].

Until title passes Customer will hold the Products on behalf of Supplier and will keep them secure, separate and intact in their original packaging.

If Customer becomes insolvent or fails to pay any sum to Supplier when due, any right of Customer to resell any Products will immediately cease and Customer will permit Supplier to enter Customer's premises and reclaim all Products whose title remains with Supplier.

6. **Defects.** Customer must inspect the Products as soon as practicable and notify Supplier in writing of any apparent defect or inconsistency with the Order within 14 days of Delivery [or, if later, 7 days after Customer is first reasonably able to inspect the Products.]

7. **Remedies.** Provided Customer has complied with 6 above Supplier will, at its sole option [and as Customer's sole remedy for any product defect,] replace any defective Products or give Customer credit for any defective Products at the Price (or any unit price per Unit specified on the Order Form.)

8. **Liability.** *[Note: The issue of seeking to exclude and/or limit liability is a highly complex area in which things are not always what they seem! – see #8.5.]* Any liability of Supplier to Customer arising out of or in connection with this agreement or the provision of Products by Supplier to Customer will be subject as follows:

a. Supplier will not be liable to Customer for any failure on the part of Supplier caused by circumstances beyond Supplier's reasonable control;

b. Nothing in this agreement will exclude or limit the liability of Supplier (1) for death or personal injury resulting from any negligence of the Supplier; or (2) arising from any fraudulent action [or gross negligence] of Supplier [or its employees or agents];

c. Subject to 8b. above, Supplier will not be liable for any indirect or consequential loss to the Customer of any kind;

d. Subject to 8b. above, the total liability of the Supplier to the Customer arising under or in connection with this agreement or the supply of Products to the Customer will not exceed [twice] the Price for the Products][*or* £[…], whichever is the lesser/greater].

9. **Insolvency**. Without limiting its other rights under the Contract, Supplier [either party] may serve written notice on Customer [the other] terminating the Order with immediate effect if Customer [the other] becomes [or indicates it is about to become] Insolvent. **Insolvent** in these Terms includes entering into bankruptcy or liquidation, or having an administrator or administrative receiver appointed or any general composition or voluntary arrangement with creditors or that the party is unable to pay its debts as [and when] they fall due.

10. **General** (*see chapter 9 for boilerplate clauses generally*)

a) *Notices – #9.4*

b) *Entire agreement – #9.5*

c) *Force majeure – #9.6*

d) *Choice of law etc. – #9.7*

e) *Severability, no waiver, variations and no third party rights –*
#9.8.

4.7 The sales chain and the different roles

As goods may pass through several hands before reaching the consumer, you need to understand where you are in the sales chain and how this might affect you. Here are some distinctions:

Manufacturer – An original producer of the goods, possibly including components from other manufacturers.

Reseller – A buyer of (normally finished) goods from a manufacturer for resale to its customers.

Distributor – A company, possibly a specialist in certain geographical or product markets, which either a) is a reseller, acquiring goods and reselling them in its own right, making its profit on the difference between the selling and buying prices (*reseller distributor*), or b) holds and transports goods on behalf of sellers (*logistics distributor*), taking fees from the seller for its services but not actually acquiring (*taking title to*) the goods.

Agent – A sales agent sells goods for a commission on behalf of a manufacturer or supplier (known in agency as the principal). A 'true' agent must not take any material level of risk on the transaction, such as the risk of customer bad debts, and must not be required to invest financially to fulfil the agency. Agents who have to invest or take risks may not be 'true' agents but be regarded as resellers, making any resale price maintenance (RPM) unlawful (#4.8).

Retailer/etailer – a seller to end users through a traditional or online store.

4.8 How do I choose between distributor and agent?

As a small business you may have the choice to be an agent or distributor or to work through one or the other; either way, there are implications. In this section distributor refers to the reseller distributor and not the logistics-only distributor, who may in fact really be an agent!

Prices and RPM

- *Distributor* – The basic rule is that producers and distributors can set prices to their own customers but cannot specify resale prices (i.e. the price charged by their customers when they sell on).

> Producers and distributors may be able to **recommend** the retail price (RRP) but generally only retailers selling direct to consumers can **stipulate** the actual retail price.

- *Agent* – Producers can however set the retail price (and prevent discounting) by selling through 'true' agents (#4.7), who don't own the goods but sell on behalf of their principals in return for commission.

Whose customers?

- *Distributor* – When a distributor sells a supplier's products to third parties, those third parties become the customers of the distributor. The supplier may get only limited customer details, and may be expected not to sell to them direct whilst the distribution agreement lasts. This can obviously slow down building a customer base.

- *Agent* – With agency the parties will agree whether agent or principal invoices the customer and/or collects payment. Either way the customers will have a direct sales relationship with the principal, which for the principal can be a more certain way of building up a loyal customer base.

Who takes the risk?

- *Distributor* – The supplier will take the risk of being paid by the distributor and the distributor takes the risk of being paid by its customers. Of course, if the distributor doesn't get paid, this could sooner or later affect its ability to pay its supplier.

- *Agents* – Provided it acts in accordance with its contract, a true agent cannot take the risk of non-payment by the customer, so this is a risk the principal must bear.

Position on termination of appointment

- *Distributor* – Distributor agreements are typically for several years, giving the parties the time to amortise the costs of setting up the new arrangements. They will often terminate at the end of the stated initial period, rolling forward afterwards until ended by, say, six months' notice either way. If the contract terms are performed, the parties probably will have no further claim against one another on termination.

- *Agent* – Most commercial agents are entitled to (non-excludable) minimum periods of notice, commission on deals negotiated before termination and termination payments designed to compensate them for the loss of the agency or the goodwill value that they have built up for the principal, either on the basis of *compensation* or an *indemnity*. Compensation is largely based on the deemed value of the agency business as a going concern at the termination date, and may be unlimited in amount; an indemnity can, if the agency agreement makes this explicit, be limited to a year's annual average commission. This cost should be factored in. As can be seen, this is a complex area where legal advice is recommended.

- *TUPE* – If employees of the agent or distributor work wholly or mainly for the customer whose contract is ending, TUPE might apply (see #5.8).

4.9 What about exclusive arrangements?

Sole and exclusive distinguished – Use these words with care. Being appointed as *sole agent*, for instance, implies that your principal won't appoint *another agent* for that product or area, but of itself that doesn't prevent the principal itself selling the same products into your area. To prevent that you'd need to be the *exclusive agent*, excluding the principal as well as other agents.

Exclusivity – If you are appointed an 'exclusive distributor' it may be assumed that your supplier won't appoint another distributor covering the same geographic or product area. Does it also mean that you can't distribute competitive products for another supplier? Absent clear language, probably not! So consider:

- Is there any kind of exclusivity in this relationship?
- If so, does it apply one way or both ways?
- And in either case, how long, how wide and how far does it go?

The contract law approach to exclusivity – Any exclusivity is also a restriction on commercial freedom, and as a starting point, the law regards such restrictions with caution. This is covered further in chapter 8 but note here the principles that any restrictions a) must be clearly spelled out and b) must be fair and proportionate – especially in extent, area and time. Go too far, and the restrictions may be unenforceable.

4.10 What is different with sales to consumers?

Introduction – The old principle of 'buyer beware' (*caveat emptor*) really no longer applies when the buyer is a consumer (#4.2), certainly in the UK and elsewhere in the EU. Regulation continues to develop with the huge growth of internet business, with seller and buyer more remote than ever. Given the extent of regulations affecting consumer sales the following can only be a brief snapshot, but note that some consumer protection laws also cover people buying for their *own business use* and that regulations also protect businesses against misleading marketing, similar to the consumer regulations mentioned below.

Website trading – The E-Commerce Directive and regulations require that when products are offered through the internet, the offer must give certain minimum details, including exactly how the offer may be accepted and when acceptance takes effect. In fact, website marketing is normally not an offer as such but an inducement for the consumer to offer to buy on the terms stated; in such cases the contract is made only when the seller accepts the consumer's offer, which may not be until a delivery date is available. Taking a consumer's money before checking that the product ordered is available may be an unfair practice or actually unlawful. Normal B2B terms of business will not be suitable; etailers should investigate this area carefully and preferably get specialist advice to ensure their website trading terms (and practices!) are legally compliant.

Some other things to consider when selling on the web:

- clear language so that consumers fully understand the implications;

- giving adequate supplier contact details and correct company or LLP details – full name, registered number, where registered and registered office (likewise on emails!);

- clarity as to who owns and what use can be made of the website content – and suitable limitation of liability provisions for user-generated or third party website content and/or links to other sites;

- consents to use personal data (#7.7).

Unfair trading – The EU Unfair Commercial Practices Directive imposed tough new rules for suppliers in relation to a wide range of consumer dealings. The emphasis is on the pre-contract trading period, requiring *sellers to be honest, open and not misleading* about what is on offer. There are at least 31 potential unfair practices listed in the UK regulations with which any business selling to consumers should familiarise itself.

> The consumer must be able to make an informed decision whether to buy a product on the terms offered. If that decision is 'materially distorted' by what the supplier does or says in its marketing, labelling or sales pitch, the consumer may be able to set the transaction aside and the supplier may be guilty of a criminal offence.

Vulnerable consumers – Further, the supplier must have regard to potential 'vulnerable' consumers, such as children or disadvantaged groups, and if necessary adapt its approach to reflect that vulnerability.

Unfair contract terms – Separate rules apply if the contract terms, for goods or services, create a 'significant imbalance' in the trading relationship between buyer and seller, 'contrary to good faith'. These rules take into account such terms as price increase clauses, unfairly limiting consumer rights to redress and one-sided compensation provisions. Offending provisions are likely to be unenforceable and the local consumer authorities (the Office of Fair Trading in the UK) may take direct action.

Liability for product safety – Defective product laws continue to tighten. Whether something is 'defective' is judged objectively and with regard to how the product is marketed, how it might be expected to be used and what instructions or warnings are given with it. Whilst warnings are laudable in intent, the risk of being sued by an injured consumer, especially in another country, probably justifies warnings on goods seemingly designed for the lowest levels of common sense.

Cancellation rights – 'Distance selling' regulations give consumers the right to cancel a sale which is made via a website or otherwise than by supplier and consumer meeting face to face. The right must be exercised within seven working days (after delivery of goods) or the date of the contract to provide services, provided the services have not already started. Goods must be returned and payment refunded within 30 days.

Consumer finance – This is a highly specialised subject on which specialist advice is recommended.

Privacy and data protection (and cookies) – If you collect any consumer details, such as email addresses, you will need to comply with the data protection and other regulations (including the need for consent to store and use personal information and to use marketing aids such as text or tracking devices stored in the consumer's hard drive, known as 'cookies').

CHAPTER 5
Supplying Services

Preliminary note: This chapter covers contracts for the supply of services by companies or self-employed people acting as service providers; it does not cover contracts of employment, which are a highly specialised area of law and practice outside the scope of this book.

5.1 How do you measure the quality of services?

The challenge – Small businesses are incredibly diverse; most probably sell services of some kind, utilising a mix of their skill, experience, contacts and labour. The law implies that those services must be provided with reasonable skill and care, both generally and at a competent level for any specialist services. So if you claim to be a specialist, you will be judged as such.

> Unlike the sale of goods, where the precise goods and price can be specified, service quality is more difficult to measure, and in each case there is the risk that service providers and their customers have different expectations or different judgments as to the standard of the work carried out.

Measuring services – Service suppliers don't normally expect to guarantee a specific result from what they do. So the challenge is to provide some measurable objectives, timescale and cost. Time and cost themselves interrelate, but what different people achieve in the same time varies greatly, as does the quality and relevance of their work. No one wants to pay more for slow work. Tests of quality need to be as objective as possible, not just the subjective opinion of each party. The benefit is a reduced risk of disputes, and all that goes with disputes. Here are some options for the parties (remembering that the small business may also be the customer):

- *Time rates* – Agree a maximum number of hours or days for a defined project (based on an agreed working day) over a stated period of time, together with a basis for the work in progress being monitored, so the customer can check (and give feedback) on any work or cost issues as things progress.

- *Milestones* – A more major project may be better broken into smaller sections with markers (*milestones*) indicating each stage to be reached, the relevant date and the payment due at that point.

- *KPIs* – Where it's possible to establish objective quality standards, pre-specified *key performance indicators (KPIs)* might be used. Failure to achieve those KPIs, either fully or to specified minimum percentage levels, could affect achievement of a milestone and/or trigger compensation or reduction in payment. KPIs do, however, need careful drafting and monitoring so that they don't become a means of oppression.

Competence – However good the personal chemistry, supplier and customer both need to think whether they are right for the job and each other. It's worth combining practical and legal approaches here, going back to your key contract objectives and making enquiries about the other party's record. If you get a defensive reply to questions, what might that be hiding? In the contract, some well-worded warranties (#8.4), for example as to the qualifications, prior experience and/or freedom from conflicting interests of the supplier, can sometimes flush out surprising information. If you are relying on a warranty, and the issue is critical, you may want to build in a right to end the contract if the warranty turns out to be false.

5.2 How long do agreements for services last?

The choice – The bigger the project and the longer its period, the greater is the risk of a mismatch of expectations arising – sooner or later. The ability to call a halt on short notice reduces the risk of things getting out of hand if expectations don't match, but can also leave each party vulnerable to the other. The supplier may have turned down substantial other work to handle this project, leaving it badly out of pocket if the customer cancels, or the customer may have other commitments resting on the result which would go wrong if the supplier just walks away. And the more personal the service or the greater the project, the more careful the parties might be about making a long-term commitment in case the relationship just doesn't work.

The two-stage approach – One approach here is a contract that makes the objectives clear but builds in flexibility that allows for inevitable changes and external events.

> There may, for instance, be a commitment to Stage 1 only, giving initial certainty on Stage 1 with an incentive for the parties to work towards Stage 2.

Such an approach can set out the Stage 2 parameters, so the intent is clear, but give each the chance of renegotiating after Stage 1. If by then they've lost faith with one another, there is probably no point in forcing them to work together, and the issue then often becomes one of damage limitation on both sides.

5.3 Do service providers have to be always available?

Absences and incapacity – Holidays (or holiday pay) are clear indicators of employment, and not to be included in contracts for services, but service providers should have some flexibility, including reasonable periods of non-availability in longer-term contracts, provided they complete the task in the allotted time. If there's a real disaster, lengthy personal incapacity of a key person might be express grounds for termination – see paragraph 8 of the sample letter agreement at #5.9.

Support and communication – Providing services is also a two-way relationship; the supplier may need some support from the customer, which is worth clarifying in the contract. For example, achieving KPIs (#5.1) may depend on the customer providing facilities such as premises and equipment for testing. Both parties need to act constructively to make things work, so regular feedback sessions on operational issues can help. Co-operation rather than confrontation may also be assisted by mechanisms such as a *change control* procedure, a process of adjustment for changes in circumstances, and *dispute escalation*, ensuring that any personal issues are referred to more senior levels where, it is hoped, a more detached view will help resolution.

5.4 Price and payment

Possible approaches – Legally it is implied that the supplier may make a reasonable charge for its services; this is somewhat vague, but a possible backstop. Clearly it's best to agree a rate or an overall fee. Again, expectations should be managed. If a supplier does extra work, the customer should not assume they won't want to be paid for it. Suppliers, for their part, should keep the customer updated with where they are on fees, and especially as to any possible variations in overall cost. At worst, the customer can then make a choice. Failure to follow these principles leads to many unnecessary disputes. If the contract is long-term, put in place some suitable review mechanism (but don't just leave this 'to be agreed' unless you provide for some form of dispute resolution if agreement is not reached).

- *Expenses* – Ensure these are covered, with any guidelines and requirements for pre-approval by the customer.

- *Payment disputes* – People are often reluctant openly to express dissatisfaction with work done.

> It's not unknown for the first complaint to come from the customer only when chased for payment, but then with a litany of alleged failures on the supplier's part.

This is where both parties will look at the contract to see just how clear it is as to exactly what work was to be done and how and when payment is due. Where appropriate, a clause requiring the customer to review the supplier's work on a regular basis, and report any issues at the time, might prevent much strife later on.

5.5 Independent contractor or employee? – The importance of the distinction

The employment and tax trap – When someone supplies services there's always a risk that they will become or may be treated as an employee of their customer. The main risks for the customer here are that this could a) give the individual employment protection rights against the customer and b) require the customer to account to the revenue authorities for PAYE income tax and national insurance (social security) contributions on the supplier's fee. For suppliers, the deduction of these taxes and contributions could be disastrous for precious cash flow. Accordingly the contract (be sure to call this a contract for services and not a service contract!) will often contain a warranty that the supplier is an independent contractor, and an indemnity from the supplier in favour of the customer to cover any additional tax the customer may be required to pay or deduct. The supplier having an existing independent business status and VAT registration will help. This is a specialist area for which professional advice is recommended, since the price of a mistake may be higher than it first appears. The following is outline guidance only:

- Suppliers should not be directors of or authorised to make management decisions for their customers.

- Any exclusivity should be carefully limited (service suppliers should generally have other customers).

- In this instance, avoid rolling contracts which suggest employment status.

- Customers should *not* generally provide specialist equipment or training to do the job, as independent suppliers will be expected to have their own skills and basic equipment.

- Control is a key test; customers should give suppliers some flexibility as to when and how to work.

- Suppliers should ideally have the ability to subcontract (but see personal services below).

- Suppliers should *not* be entitled to customer company benefits (overtime, sick pay etc.).

Personal services – The no-subcontracting test may be problematic where customers hire specific people. They don't want to hire Jones and have Smith turn up instead. The law recognises 'personal' contracts, where suppliers cannot transfer their rights to someone else unless the customer agrees, but if you require a specific person, it's worth specifying that in the contract (see para 8 in #5.9 and also assignment/sub-contracting in #9.2).

Agency workers and interns – Temporary workers might also be entitled to *workers' rights*, available to UK agency workers, including the use of staff facilities and equal treatment with employees. There are also rules regarding interns, work experience placements and some voluntary workers, with minimum wage and other employment-type protection potentially applying. These rules are obviously less likely to apply to those truly self-employed as described above.

Contracting with a company as supplier – Many service suppliers are limited companies, sometimes as a tax vehicle for the individual.

> If an individual supplier's personal commitment is important, ask the individual to be an additional party to the contract.

With bigger service providers, the continued availability of a named employee (or team) might be important, but the issue is trickier. If the customer insists on being able to terminate the contract if the individual or team cease to be available, this might give the named employees an unacceptably high degree of leverage over the service provider, probably something for the latter to avoid.

5.6 Confidentiality, intellectual property and restrictive covenants

Suppliers and customers are understandably focused on what needs to be done to complete the job and settle payment, yet what happens afterwards to the product or the services can be just as important in the long run. These issues are dealt with in some detail in chapters 7 and 8, but you should think from the outset about the longer term, and especially:

- what confidentiality obligations exist and for how long;

- who has rights in what has been and is being developed; and

- how far the parties are free to compete with one another now and in the future.

5.7 Outsourcing

Outsourcing is a major industry in logistics, IT, human resources, information management, contract management and many other areas. Although many outsourcing companies are huge operations, small businesses may be well placed to offer outsourced services in specialist areas or may themselves benefit from outsourcing. Since outsourcing means delegating a vital function to the service provider it is likely to involve a major information-gathering and set-up exercise. As a result, to give parties the chance to amortise their respective set-up costs, outsourcing contracts typically are for longer terms with detailed KPIs and/or other quality standards. The area is complex legally, so specialist advice is recommended on the contract.

> Because delegating a vital part of your business to someone else carries major risks of something going wrong, outsourcing negotiations will need to concentrate on the end of the relationship almost as much as the beginning.

For example, termination periods should give adequate time for the work to return in-house or a replacement operation to take over. Such contracts are often the subject of tenders, with the key terms set out by the customer in the *invitation to tender (ITT)* or similar document, which may in turn form part of the contract.

5.8 Transfer of employment – TUPE

What is TUPE? – TUPE stands for the *Transfer of Undertakings (Protection of Employment) Regulations, derived from the Acquired Rights Directive* which applies across the EU. It's an area where specialist advice is essential.

The aim of TUPE is laudable, to ensure that those whose job effectively transfers from one business to another business keep their jobs and maintain their employment terms. The practice however is fraught with complications.

To understand when and how TUPE might be relevant let's consider an example.

Elaine is an IT specialist employed by *Unlimited Things Limited (UTL)*. UTL decides to outsource its IT operation to *Gizmos* PLC. The IT operation is a largely self-contained part of UTL, Elaine's work for that department comprises the majority of what she does for UTL and the same outsourced role in Gizmos will include dealing with UTL as a customer.

In these circumstances, by virtue of TUPE, once the outsourcing goes live Elaine's employment will automatically transfer to Gizmos on the same terms and conditions (including continuity of service) as she had with UTL. Moreover, with limited exceptions, any attempt to change that arrangement (e.g. by UTL trying to make Elaine redundant before the 'transfer' or Gizmos changing her employment terms by 'harmonising' her pay with any lower benefits of Gizmos' staff) is liable to be deemed automatic unfair dismissal of Elaine.

- TUPE and associated regulations contain extensive obligations to ensure that Elaine and any other UTL employees liable to be affected by changes (i.e. not just those transferring) are informed and consulted *before* the transfer or any changes take place, with compensation payable for non-compliance.

- Generally TUPE makes the transferee, Gizmos in this example, liable for any errors and compensation payable. Gizmos therefore needs to ensure it gets correct information and assistance from UTL in good time. There are likely to be extensive TUPE warranties and indemnities between UTL and Gizmos in the outsourcing contract.

- Elaine is legally entitled to refuse to transfer to Gizmos but if she refuses her employment with UTL will end without any entitlement to compensation or redundancy payment. Alternatively UTL could (but are not obliged to) offer Elaine another role within UTL or may (even if not obliged to do so) offer her a redundancy payment if she did not wish to transfer.

- If Elaine stays in post with Gizmos, but UTL later takes the operation back in-house or transfers it to another outsourcing specialist (*second-generation outsourcing*), Elaine's employment, if mainly geared to looking after UTL, would transfer back to UTL (or on to the new outsource provider) on the same terms as she had with Gizmos at the time of this later transfer.

Thinking ahead – This, it should be stressed, is just a simplified scenario. Those starting small businesses may well have experienced TUPE already. Elaine might, for example, have decided to leave Gizmos when she realised what might happen and to start her own business doing part of UTL's IT work. If she succeeds and takes on staff, those staff could transfer to UTL or another provider if she ever lost the IT contract herself. So if she does succeed and expand, she might want to think carefully – and take advice in good time – as to whether or how she could retain her key people if such circumstances ever arose for her.

5.9 A contract for services

Two different approaches are set out below. The first shows a traditional form of contract (albeit in modern style) and the second illustrates how similar issues can be covered in a shorter letter form. The first example does not seek to cover any detailed IT issues and is provided essentially as a reference point for the layout of a formal contract. The letter form example, which has some aspects omitted but deals with others in more detail, assumes that Elaine, referred to above, is in this case a genuine self-employed person providing services to UTL (as opposed to being an employee transferring under TUPE). Note, however, that both formats ignore any more detailed software or system development provisions, are subject to the comments earlier in this chapter and to the explanatory comments elsewhere in this book and, as with other examples, are subject to the caveats section in the introduction.

Example 1: IT services agreement

DATE:

PARTIES:

(1) *[Full personal or correct registered company name]* **Limited** (registered in [England] with number [company number if appropriate] of [or whose registered office is at] [address] (**Client**); and

(2) **[Full personal or registered company name]** [(registered in [England] with number [company number if appropriate]) of [or whose registered office is at] [address] (**Supplier**).

BACKGROUND

(A)   Supplier is a provider of IT services.

(B)   [Following completion of a satisfactory pilot project] Client has requested and Supplier has agreed to provide [further] services on the terms set out in this agreement.

1 Definitions and Interpretation

1.1   In this agreement a) the words and expressions set out in clause 1.2 have the meanings shown opposite them; b) references to legislation and regulations are to include that legislation or regulation as amended and in force from time to time; c) the singular includes the plural, the masculine the feminine and company includes all forms of incorporated and unincorporated legal entity and vice versa in each case; d) clause headings are for convenience only and not to be used to interpret this agreement and e) references to a party (other than a third party), clause, or schedule are to a party, clause or schedule to or in this agreement.

1.2   Defined terms

Associated Company	any company under the Control of the relevant party or any third party that controls it; *[if applicable]*
Charges	the charges payable by Client for the Services, as set out in clause 4;
Commencement Date	*[insert date services are due to start]*;
Confidential Information	the terms of this agreement and any information relating to the business of either party or otherwise of a confidential nature, excluding any information a) previously known to that party or b) generally published or available to the public except (in either case) where disclosure results from breach of confidentiality; *[alternative definitions of confidential information are given in other examples]*
Control	the ability to direct the affairs of a company or other corporate body at shareholder or management level;

Deliverables	any materials specified in the Schedule or which the parties otherwise agree in writing that Supplier will provide to Client;
Intellectual Property Rights	rights in patents, designs, copyright, database rights, trademarks, trade and business names, in each case registered or unregistered, all applications to register any of them, and all equivalent rights anywhere in the world;
Services	the services described in [clause 3.2/the Schedule];
Term	the period of this agreement from the Commencement Date until the end date set out in clause 2 or earlier Termination;
Termination	the date on which this agreement comes to an end for any reason.

2   Term

2.1   This agreement commences on the Commencement Date and, unless terminated earlier in accordance with its terms, will end on [date].

3   Supplier's obligations

3.1   Supplier will provide the Services and supply the Deliverables in a professional manner and within any agreed timescales, in accordance with the Client's reasonable directions, best market practice, all applicable laws and regulations and the terms of this agreement.

3.2   Supplier will *[set out Supplier's main obligations here in sufficient detail, distinguishing between absolute obligations ('the Supplier will [do x and y]') and endeavours obligations ('the Supplier will use best/reasonable endeavours to [do x and y]'). The detail description of the services, including where and how they are to be supplied, can be included here or in the schedule.*

3.3   Supplier will report to and consult with Client as to the most effective provision of the Services and Deliverables as reasonably requested by Client in accordance with this agreement.

Supplier will not, during the Term [set out any negative obligations] …

4   Payment

4.1   Supplier will charge Client [the sum of £[…] per [hour/day/week/month] for the provision of the Services [with a minimum of £[…] per day/week/month and a maximum of £[…] per day/week/month] and Client will pay Supplier the Charges, together with any applicable VAT, within [30] days of receiving Supplier's valid tax invoice. These amounts will be in full payment for the Services and the Client will have no liability for any further amounts except to the extent [set out in clause 4.2 and] previously approved in writing by Client.

4.2   Client will pay Supplier any reasonable costs and expenses previously approved in writing by Client wholly incurred by Supplier in performing the Services.

5   Liability *[Note: a reminder that this is a highly complex area – see #8.5]*

5.1   Nothing in this agreement will limit the liability of either party a) for death or personal injury resulting from any negligence of the other party; b) arising from any fraudulent action [or gross negligence]; c) any [indemnity or] breach by either party of any obligation of confidentiality under this agreement.

5.2   Subject to clause 5.1, neither party will be liable for any indirect or consequential loss of any kind arising out of or in connection with this agreement.

5.3   [Subject to clause 5.1 the total liability of either party to the other arising under or in connection with this agreement or the provision of the Services to the Client (other than the Client's obligation to pay the Charges) will not exceed £[…].

This limitation will not apply to any liability under clause 6 (Intellectual Property Rights) or clause 8 (Confidentiality).]

6   Intellectual Property

6.1   Client owns and will own the Intellectual Property Rights in any Deliverables and accordingly Supplier hereby assigns (including by way of current and future assignment of copyright) and agrees to assign to Client all its Intellectual Property Rights in the Deliverables. Supplier will sign all documents and do all other things necessary to give effect to this clause. *[Drafting note: this may need to be limited to IPR specific to the named Client only if the Deliverables include material used by Supplier generally or for other clients.]*

6.2   Supplier warrants to Client that provision of the Services and Deliverables under this agreement will not infringe the Intellectual Property Rights or otherwise breach any legal rights of any third party. Supplier will give all reasonable assistance to and indemnify Client against any losses, damages or costs suffered or incurred by Client [or any Associated Company of Client] in relation to any third party claim against Client [or any Associated Company of Client] arising from breach or alleged breach of this warranty (Claim) but only to the extent that Client notifies Supplier as soon as practicable on becoming aware of the Claim and Supplier has full conduct of the Claim through its professional advisers, keeping Client fully informed and consulted on the progress, handling and any potential settlement of the Claim.

7   Termination

7.1   Either party may terminate this agreement immediately on written notice to the other party if the other either a) commits a material breach of this agreement and, where that breach is capable of remedy, fails to remedy it within 14 days of written notice from the non-breaching party specifying the breach and requiring it to be remedied; or b) becomes insolvent or unable to pay his or its debts as and when they fall due. Either party may also terminate this agreement immediately on written notice to the other party within [two] months of first becoming aware that the other party has undergone a change of Control.

7.2   On Termination Supplier will promptly deliver to Client all Deliverables, including any work in progress.

7.3   *[Set out any post-Termination restrictive covenants]*

7.4   Termination will not affect the previously accrued rights or liabilities of the parties under this agreement or any provision expressed or intended to have effect after Termination.

8   Confidentiality

8.1   Each party agrees to keep the Confidential Information confidential and not to disclose it except: a) with the other party's prior written approval; b) where required by law or by a regulatory body having jurisdiction over it; or c) to the party's professional advisers on a 'need to know basis' and on terms of strict confidentiality.

9   General

9.1   *Notices:* Any notice or other communication under this agreement a) must be in writing delivered personally or sent by [first class post], [or sent by email with a delivery receipt] to the relevant party's address as below or as last notified to the other; b) is deemed to have been given on the day it is delivered personally, or on the second day following the date it was sent by [first class] post [or on the next working day following transmission by email].

9.2   *Entire agreement and non-reliance:* This agreement [and any documents referred to in it] constitutes the entire agreement between the parties, and supersedes all other agreements or arrangements between the parties (whether written or oral, express or implied), relating to the subject matter of this agreement. Each party accepts that it is relying entirely on the terms set out in this agreement and not on any pre-contract statement or representation made by any other party except to the extent (if at all) specifically set out in this agreement.

9.3   *Force majeure:* Neither party will be liable for any failure to perform or delay in performing any obligation under this agreement (other than a payment obligation) for circumstances beyond its reasonable control providing that it promptly notifies the other party of such circumstances and uses its reasonable endeavours to mitigate their effects on this agreement. If such circumstances continue to prevent performance for more than [60] days, either party may terminate this agreement on 30 days' written notice to the other.

9.4   *Assignment:* [This agreement is personal to the Supplier, who may not assign, transfer or subcontract its/his/her rights or obligations under this agreement] – or – [Neither party may assign or transfer its rights or obligations under this agreement without the prior written consent of the other party [, such consent not to be unreasonably withheld or delayed]]. [This clause will not prevent the assignment or transfer of rights or obligations to an Associated Company.] Subject to the above, this agreement is binding upon each party's successors and assigns and personal representatives, as the case may be.

9.5   *Severability:* Any provision of this agreement which is held to be illegal or unenforceable will, to the extent necessary, be omitted from this agreement. The enforceability of the remainder will not be affected.

9.6   *Waivers:* No party will be affected by any delay or failure in exercising or any partial exercising of its rights under this agreement unless it has signed an express written waiver or release.

9.7   *Variations:* No variations of this agreement are effective unless made in writing signed by the parties or their authorised agents.

9.8   *Right of third parties:* The parties intend that no term of this agreement may be enforced by any person who is not a party to it.

9.9   *Law and jurisdiction*: This agreement will be governed and interpreted in accordance with [the laws of England and Wales] and the parties submit to the [exclusive] jurisdiction of the [English] courts.

SCHEDULE – further description of the Services/Deliverables

[Insert here a reasonable list/description of the Services in numbered or bullet points with any conditions so as to be able to judge whether or not the Services are being performed according to the contract.]

Signed by:

for and on behalf of

[Client] Limited

Address for service of notices: *[business address + email address if applicable + person to be addressed]*

Signed by:

[for and on behalf of:]

[Supplier] [Limited]

Address for service of notices: *[business address + email address if applicable + person to be addressed]*

Example 2: Letter agreement

Dear Elaine

IT Services

This letter confirms our agreement for you to provide services to us as follows:

1. *Services* – The services (**Services**) will be *[set out detail with sufficient clarity as per comments above]*.

2. *Term* – You will perform the Services from *[date]* to *[date]*. We may continue arrangements after then but only if we both agree.

3. *Location* – You will carry out the services from your own workplace but will attend our offices at *[address]* one morning each week as agreed with us (save for reasonable or unavoidable absences as pre-notified to us) to *[e.g. review the performance and resilience of our IT security systems]*.

4. *Fees* – We will pay you a fee of £[...] per month for the Services within 30 days of our receipt of your invoice, plus VAT if applicable. We will at the same time reimburse you, on receipt of the appropriate vouchers, for any expenses previously approved by us which you have incurred wholly in providing the Services.

5. *Assistance* – We will provide remote access for you personally to such of our systems as you may reasonably need to perform the Services. When you attend our offices we will provide you with a suitable temporary workstation and facilities appropriate to your needs.

6. *Confidentiality* – You will during the period of this agreement and for two years after it ends keep confidential and not copy or disclose to any other person or company all information that you receive or access relating to this company, its directors, employees, agents, customers and all others with whom it deals, including (without limitation) all financial or trading information, product or marketing plans, proposals, prices, margins and the like (**Confidential Information**). This obligation will not affect such information as a) has become public knowledge without any breach of confidence on your part or b) you can show that you lawfully held before commencing the Services or c) you are lawfully required to disclose to any regulatory authorities. When this agreement ends you will return to us any Confidential Information in document form and certify that any Confidential Information has been deleted from all your IT systems.

7.   *IPR* – Each of us agrees that the other may access and use the technology systems of the other only so far as properly and reasonably required to perform and review performance of the Services but will have no other rights of any kind to any intellectual property **(IP)** in the systems of the other or their respective content. However, if you create any IP specifically for us in the course of the Services, you agree that this will become exclusively our IP and you will at our request assign to us all your rights in it without further compensation.

8.   *Agreement personal* – You will perform the Services personally and this agreement will be personal to each of us. Accordingly our respective rights and obligations may not be assigned or sub-contracted without the other's consent, except that you may, if unable to perform the Services for reasons beyond your personal control or if we otherwise agree, engage another person reasonably acceptable to us to do so for a period not exceeding [four] weeks provided that a) such person agrees with and undertakes to us in writing in equivalent terms to those set out in paragraphs 6 and 7 above and b) that if you are unable to perform the Services yourself for more than [four] weeks continuously or in any period of six months we [or either of us] may terminate this agreement by immediate written notice to you [or the other].

9.   *Termination* – Either of us may terminate this agreement by serving written notice on the other if the other commits a material breach of this agreement which it fails to remedy within 21 days of written notice specifying the breach and requiring its remedy or if the other becomes insolvent. Specifically a failure on your part to *[specify any key elements]* on time on more than [one/two] occasion(s) in any [six] months' period will be deemed a material breach incapable of remedy.

10.   *Self-employed status* – You warrant to us that you are self-employed and will indemnify us against all taxation, national insurance, interest, costs and similar liabilities we may be called upon to pay in relation to the fees and expenses paid or payable to you under this agreement.

I hope this covers everything. If you agree, please sign and return the duplicate of this letter to me as soon as you can and in any event before [date]. We all look forward to working [*or* continuing our work] with you.

Yours sincerely

U.T. Lehman

Director for and on behalf of Unlimited Things Limited

5.10 Event planning scenario and examples

To see the principles summarised so far in another context, imagine your business involves organising events and you want to use your own contracts to keep things consistent and to try to manage risk.

If you hire a venue you'll probably have to agree to sign the contract largely as provided by the venue owners. You'd want to see what level of risk that leaves you with and how you could best manage that risk with your own contract for those providing services to or at the event.

Here's a basic example, this time using the approach of an order form plus standard terms. There are many variables possible on various issues, depending on your own attitude to risk, a subject considered further in chapter 8. A key issue here will be cancellation; what if the event is called off, or postponed, or if your supplier cancels or fails to turn up? How far do you go in trying to cover these risks? How tough – or one-sided in your negotiations – do you want to be? Or would you rather keep quiet about the risk and deal with it if and when it happens?

For example, para 2.1 gives the option of providing an endeavours obligation (see #3.10) as opposed to an absolute obligation, since the customer here may not control the venue or the venue contract may have its own limitations on commitment. The same point applies to paras 3.2, 6.2, and 6.3, where there are various options as to cancellation, perhaps one of the most foreseeable risks in such contracts. The time period to insert will vary according to the degree of preparation required and the likely availability of alternative contractors. Some contracts will have a one-sided right to cancel with impunity; others will have absolute obligations with no right to cancel at all.

Paragraph 4 covers other key areas, confidentiality and IP, already mentioned in this chapter and followed up in chapter 7. Are special designs or products or artwork being prepared for the event, and, if so, who should they belong to afterwards and how else might they be used? Can the event be photographed or recorded and, if so, how might the pictures or recording be used or what limitations should be imposed? This will all need some thought. Photos for example raise several issues. If you hire a photographer for an event, who will have the right to use and/or sell the photos? Quite apart from copyright, what issues of privacy could come into play if the event is expected to be private? If you are buying the right to use photos, you'll generally need the consent of the photographer, assuming they are still the copyright owner, and should ensure you have covered the ownership of and risk in the photos (as opposed to the copyright), the permitted term (sometimes limited, say, to a year), territory (possibly limited to UK) and form of reproduction (e.g. digital/online as well as physical if appropriate), the need for attribution and possibly even the number of copies that may be made.

Agreement for Services

(This agreement comprises this Order Form and the Standard
Terms set out overleaf)

Order Form

Parties	(1) […] of […] (**Supplier, you,** or **your**) (2) […] of […] (**Customer, we,** us or **our**)
Services to be provided by Supplier	*Set out sufficient detail of the services to cover all major aspects with enough clarity to decide if they have been adequately performed.*
Facilities to be provided by Customer	*Set out any specific facilities for the Customer to provide, such as microphones, stage accessories etc.*
Relevant Date(s)	*Date or dates of the planned event including any specific pre-event occasions.*
Event and Event Location	
Travel	*Set out details of any travel etc. arrangements which it is for the Customer to provide – and relevant levels – e.g. on aircraft or trains.*
Fee	*The total fee and any stage or follow-up payments.*
Signatures	.... **Supplier** **Customer**
Date	

Standard Terms *(normally best set out on the reverse of the order form)*

1. Obligations of Supplier

1.1   You will provide the Services at and preparatory to the Event with reasonable skill and care.

1.2   You will comply with all applicable laws and regulations applicable to the provision of the Services and as may be communicated to you in relation to the Event or the Event Location.

1.3   *[Other specifics]*

2. Obligations of Customer

2.1   We will [use our reasonable endeavours to] provide a suitable venue and Facilities for the Event at the Event Location on the Relevant Date(s).

2.2   We will use our reasonable endeavours to [have the owner of the Event venue/organiser of the Event] obtain all necessary licences and comply with all applicable laws and regulations applicable to the holding of the Event and the suitability of the Event Location.

3. Term and agreement and cancellation rights

3.1   This agreement will continue during the Event and thereafter so long as its terms are applicable.

3.2   Subject to clauses 6.2 and 6.3 either party may cancel this agreement [for any reason] on written notice to the other received no later than [21] days before the Event Date.

4. Confidentiality, Intellectual Property and Communications

4.1   You will, during the period of this agreement and for two years after the Event Date, keep confidential (and not copy or disclose to any other person or company) all information that you receive or access relating to us, our directors, employees, agents, customers and all others with whom we deal, including (without limitation) all financial or trading information, product or marketing plans, proposals, prices, margins and the like (**Confidential Information**). This obligation will not affect such information as a) has become public knowledge without any breach of confidence on your part or b) you can show that you lawfully held before commencing the Services or c) you are lawfully required to disclose to any regulatory authorities. When this agreement ends you will return to us any Confidential Information in document form and certify that any Confidential Information has been deleted from all your IT systems.

4.2   You will not, without our prior written consent, record or communicate in any form to any third party [your involvement in the Event – or – other than the fact of your involvement in the Event] any details or extracts or other information or material from or relating to the Event or those attending the Event.

4.3   All intellectual property rights of any kind created or devised specifically by us or by you for us or for the Event or relating to or arising in the course of the Event (**Customer IPR**) will belong to us absolutely. You will not reproduce or display any such material in any form at any time without our prior written consent and will, if and when so requested by us, assign to us without cost any intellectual property rights you may have in such Customer IPR. This clause will not affect your rights in any intellectual property created or devised by you at other times and for other purposes.

4.4   You will be responsible for and indemnify us against a) any breach by you or anyone acting on your behalf of any of the provisions of this paragraph 4 or b) any third party claim made or liability awarded against us or any employee, agent or licensee of ours arising out of any material or the use of any material supplied by you and used by us at or in connection with the Event, except to the extent, if at all, that such claim or liability arises from our own negligence or breach of any of our material obligations under this agreement. *[Note: see also the alternative warranty and indemnity clause example at #8.4.]*

4.5   The provisions of this paragraph 4 will continue to apply after and notwithstanding cancellation or termination of this agreement.

5.   Travel and other arrangements

You will make all your own travel and subsistence arrangements except as otherwise stated under Travel in the Order Form.

6.   Payment

6.1   We will pay you in total for the Services the Fee set out in the Order Form and any applicable VAT within [30] days [from end of the month] after receiving your invoice following the Event.

6.2   If the Event is cancelled [for reasons beyond our control] [and we notify you to that effect no later than [21] days before the Event Date] we will have no liability to you for or in relation to the Fee. If we cancel this agreement by written notice to you before the Event Date [for any other reason] or less than [21] days before the Event Date, the Fee will be reduced by half.

6.3   You may cancel this agreement for [any] reason[s] [beyond your control] by notice in writing to us received by us no later than [21] days before the Event Date. [If you cancel otherwise you accept that we will need to engage another supplier to provide the Services, possibly at higher cost, and accordingly you agree to indemnify us against any extra costs we may incur in so doing.]

7.   Limitations of liability

7.1   We will have no liability to you for the Fee or otherwise if the Event Location becomes unavailable for the Event for any reason outside our control.

7.2   Neither party will be liable to the other for failure for any reason to perform any obligation under this agreement (other than an obligation to make payment) due to an event beyond the control of that party.

7.3 Neither party will be liable to the other for any indirect or consequential loss caused to the other. Any other liability of either party to the other for any breach of this agreement or any act or neglect related to this agreement (other than any express indemnity set out in this agreement) will be limited to [twice the amount of the Fee].

7.4 *[Entire agreement and non-reliance clause – see #9.5.]*

Termination

[See the wording and notes in #10.4.]

Termination of this agreement will not affect any clauses or provisions of this agreement expressed or intended to have effect after termination.

8.   General

[Boilerplate etc. clauses – See #9.2 to 9.8 inclusive.]

CHAPTER 6
Payment Terms

6.1 The contract price

The basics – Getting the price right and getting paid are fundamentals for anyone supplying goods or services. For the customer, whilst headline price is often negotiated early on, the overall cost and payment terms may be just as significant, and the significance will increase with longer-term contracts and more volatile markets. As with everything else, the key to price is first of all being clear what you have ordered or agreed to supply.

Goods – Price is initially straightforward when the number of products and the price per product are specified, preferably with a total payable. The buyer should check whether the seller's terms of business (#4.4) apply and, if so, whether these contain any chargeable extras, such as delivery or commissioning charges.

Services and approvals – As seen in the previous chapter, fees are likely to be on a day or other rate basis and/or an overall fee. What happens if the job turns out to be more complex or takes longer than expected?

> Where fees are directly related to time spent, customers will sensibly want the contract to require approval of any excess over the basic fee and/or specify a maximum fee (with the risk that this becomes a target for the supplier to work towards).

There is a distinction between extra work that is needed but was wholly unexpected, which probably justifies a fair extra charge, and work that the supplier could have foreseen but simply didn't allow for, which the supplier might bear. If service providers offer fixed fees they might want express obligations or customer warranties in the contract as to the essential support they'll need from the customer to achieve their targets. Approval may also be required for expenses (see examples at para 4 in #5.9).

Sales tax/VAT – UK consumer prices must generally be quoted *inclusive* of VAT, whereas in the USA and some other countries sales tax may be added at point of sale. So any reference to consumer price needs to be clear on taxes. Most B2B business contracts quote prices ex-VAT, so it's wise to have such contracts state explicitly that prices are quoted exclusive of VAT (or other applicable sales tax), which will be payable in addition on production of the supplier's valid VAT invoice.

6.2 What about price variations?

With consumer internet sales any right for the seller to raise the price materially will probably be an unfair (and unenforceable) contract term unless the customer is given the right to cancel if the price goes up, either at all or above a specified level. With B2B, there are other alternatives, including:

- *Limiting any increase* – to a specified percentage, either overall or in any period;

- *Requiring minimum periods of notice* – before any increase takes effect and/or limiting the dates from which increases can apply (giving some certainty to the customer's resales);

- *Linking the increase to a specified retail or consumer price index* – possibly with a maximum percentage; if the formula is complex, a worked example can be highly beneficial in ensuring mutual understanding at negotiation stage!

- *Building in a customer cancellation right* – either in any event or if the increase is above an agreed percentage;

- *Permitting either party to call for a review* – thus up or down, especially with volatile commodity prices;

- *Third party reference* – using an agreed index or an independent industry expert to fix the price, specifying the person or body in question or who nominates them if the parties cannot agree whom to select.

6.3 Payment date and credit periods

Due date – Credit is a huge problem for many small businesses, with big business often paying late and suppliers reluctant to offend by charging interest. New European Commission-originated rules applying from 2012/13 assume (in the absence of other agreement) that payment is due 30 days from receipt of invoice or, if later, receipt or acceptance of the goods or services. If the credit period is specified it may not exceed 60 days (30 days with a public body as customer) unless certain tests are fulfilled. Moreover, it will not be possible to exclude these rules by the contract. In the meantime, and in any case to avoid uncertainty, the contract should set out at least:

- *the due date* – the date by which payment is to be made (e.g. 'by no later than [date]');

- *the payment method* – how payment is to be made (e.g. 'by direct transfer in cleared funds to the Supplier's bank account *[add appropriate details]*'); – potentially very valuable for certainty and cash flow – and

- *position on default* – what happens if it is not paid on time.

Credit periods – These can vary widely between industries, also depending on the creditworthiness of the customer. If you are told 'payment 30 days', check whether this means 30 days from the date of invoice or 30 days from the end of the month in which the supplier received the invoice, which could in some cases effectively double the credit period.

Remember that the longer the credit period, the later you know about problems and the greater the risk of non-payment. The more in the queue ahead of you, the less your chances of getting paid if there is not enough to go around.

6.4 What about failure to pay?

Interest – If there is no other adequate remedy in the contract the law implies an obligation on a business paying late to pay interest at a high rate on the overdue amount. Although suppliers may fear the market consequences, this may be enforced and the new rules will mean interest becoming *automatically due* and suppliers having the right to recover fixed compensation plus recovery fees. It also seems likely that attempts to avoid interest or compensation will be regarded as unfair. In practice it is still best for both parties to agree and honour a sensible interest payment, such as interest on any amount due and unpaid from the due date to the date of payment at around 3 or 4 percentage points above a stated major bank base rate.

'All sums due' – Some contracts contain a provision that if *any* payment is in arrears, all amounts payable under the contract become automatically due, carrying interest in their turn. Such wording needs to be watched carefully. It's one thing to say that any credit already given is cancelled – fair enough if one payment is missed – but quite another to require the defaulter then to pay up everything that *may become due* in the rest of the contract period.

Written notice and grace periods – The customer might want a short 'grace' period before interest is charged, to avoid being liable for interest unless it has received notice of non-payment. Suppliers frequently resist this, as it effectively puts the onus back on the supplier. It is still worth pressing, however, for contractual entitlement to notice of non-payment before any *breach action* is taken, even if the remedy period for non-payment is as short as seven days.

Recovery action – If payment is not made as the contract requires, the 'innocent' party can sue to recover what's due, which could add court fees and legal costs, as well as interest, to the debt. This can be done irrespective of any right to terminate the contract.

Persistent failure to pay – Some companies persistently pay late, creating great aggravation for suppliers. One option here is for the contract to provide for persistent non-payment (say more than two breaches in any 12 months) as cause for termination. Enforcement may risk the future relationship, but the right at least gives the supplier some sanction.

Set-off and counterclaim – Another resource (or ploy, according to your viewpoint) is a unilateral deduction for alleged short delivery or quality issues. Whether or not the contract contains an express right of set-off, and unless there is evidence of potential insolvency of the creditor (see below), such action should really be limited to occasions when the payer has informed the supplier/customer of the query and has exhausted reasonable opportunities to resolve any dispute. A clause prohibiting set-off might assist, but would still need to be enforced and could also backfire if for any reason the roles were reversed.

6.5 Some contracts provide for royalties – how does that work?

When royalties may be payable – The position is perhaps best illustrated by a theoretical example, although it should be noted that royalty provisions can be much more complex than this example!

- Sam is a freelance writer. He writes regular columns for a magazine and a newspaper for fixed fees and also occasional pieces for other publications. These are covered by simple agreements dealing primarily with copyright (#7.5) plus invoicing and payment of the fee.

- Sam is also now working on a book, and has received a modest advance from a publisher on signing a publishing agreement. He will also be entitled to royalties as a percentage of the RRP of the book or the net sums received by the publisher, according to the type of book and market in which it is sold (and Sam should be clear which, since the market rates and the net effect can be quite different). The advance is an advance payment of royalties, non-recoverable by the publisher if the book doesn't sell, with royalties becoming payable only once the advance is 'recouped'. If Sam's advance is £5,000, this means that £5,000 of royalties will have to accrue to Sam's royalty account before the publishers pay him anything more.

- Royalties are typically calculated and paid once or twice a year, based on sales made up to the end of a yearly or half-yearly period ending three months before. The royalty statement will include the number and/or sales value of books sold in the period.

- Royalties may be affected by withholding tax if paid to a rights holder based outside the UK.

- An audit clause should enable Sam to call for an independent accountant to examine the publisher's accounts to verify the sales and royalties, with any necessary adjustment then being made good.

6.6 Credit risk

It's a commonplace that 'cash is king', with many smaller businesses forced to spend undue time chasing cash flow. But, as we well know, the size of a company is no guarantee it can pay its debts and the larger companies are, the harder they can fall. So it pays for the growing business also to do credit checks on its major customers, both before the contract is signed and as it progresses, keeping a careful eye open for any payment 'slippage'. The warning signs are often noticeable before the event and general vigilance can help identify the risk level. This should at least enable a positive choice to be made as to whether or how far to continue; the blind faith of creditors is as dangerous as the blind faith of those who carry on their business when all hope is gone. Credit insurance may help to alleviate some risk, but obviously only where available and at a cost.

6.7 Personal guarantees

Trading without limited liability – If you are a sole trader or partnership, but have not incorporated as a limited liability company or LLP (#3.4), you will be personally liable for all your business debts.

> Notwithstanding tax issues you should always think what level of risk you are facing and whether it is wiser to use a limited company for all or the riskier part of your operations so as to insulate your personal assets.

Be aware of the risk – Directors of small companies may be asked for personal guarantees. If asked, think hard; don't assume it will never happen or that people will go easy on you. The people you'll deal with if your business can't pay will not be the same as those you dealt with when all was well. The loss of a business is hard enough to bear but losing personal assets and perhaps your home can place intolerable strains on even the strongest. If a personal guarantee becomes inevitable, think of the following:

- *Limit the liability* – under the guarantee to a specified maximum amount that would be painful for you but which you could ultimately pay (without recourse to the company), including interest if possible, and with some time to pay.

- *Fix the period of guarantee or secure a right to terminate* – Limit the guarantee period, say to six or twelve months maximum or insist on the right to bring the guarantee to an end on, say, one month's notice. This would not cancel existing liability but would stop your liability for future debts of the business. Ending a guarantee might well prejudice your business, but at least it will stop the debt rising.

- *Insist on being notified personally* – immediately the company fails to pay.

- *Amount due* – Require proper evidence or an independent reference if you challenge the amount claimed.

- *Control* – Beware giving any guarantee if you are not in control – and plan to stay in control – of the company you guarantee. If you are a minority shareholder or partner, you will be vulnerable to being outvoted or forced out but remain guaranteeing the business. If you are a joint owner, try to have guarantee obligations shared and ideally split severally with other joint owners. Make sure that your respective liabilities are set out in writing and remember that if the guarantee is given *jointly and severally*, the creditor can come after *any of the guarantors for the full amount*, leaving the one who can or does pay to recover their contributions from their co-guarantors.

- *Change of control* – If you think you might sell your business in the future, insert a clause that your guarantee will be released if a reasonable alternative guarantor is offered. You can then insist that anyone buying your company puts up their own guarantor. There is otherwise no legal obligation on the beneficiary of a guarantee to agree this.

6.8 Insolvency

Types of insolvency – The main ones now are:

Insolvent liquidation/winding up/bankruptcy – Liquidation is the death of a limited company. It ceases trading, the directors lose office and a *qualified insolvency practitioner (QIP)* takes over to call in the debts and pay out the creditors in their due priority. That puts the taxman first to some extent, but will favour anyone holding registered security, which probably means the bank. Unsecured creditors rarely receive much more than a single figure percentage of the total debt due to them. Bankruptcy is the equivalent for the individual.

Administration / Chapter 11 (in USA) – This is a kind of suspended animation, often used where the company cannot continue as it is but there is the chance of a rescue or prospects of getting more for the creditors than if the company went down immediately. In this case the directors can carry on the business in accordance with an agreed plan under the supervision of a QIP. Debtors have to pay their debts as normal but creditors are held at bay, and can neither force repayment nor collect their goods under ROT provisions (#4.6). Sometimes the business is sold, perhaps taking on employees and doing deals with creditors providing essential supplies. After administration the company normally goes into liquidation but occasionally is restored to health.

CVA (companies) or IVA (individuals) – VA stands for voluntary arrangement, a slightly less formal way of securing an agreement with the majority of secured creditors and a large majority of the unsecured creditors. There is a formal process and agreement under which the company continues, but again under close supervision.

If the ship is sinking

> If your company is potentially insolvent don't carry on when all around you think the hope is gone. Get early professional advice from someone who knows the ropes and the rules.

If your company does go into insolvent liquidation the directors' prior conduct will be scrutinised by the QIP, who can:

- *Liability* – order the directors to pay into the company money lost by creditors if, for example, the company pays some creditors in unfair preference to others, sells assets well below market value or carries on trading after the point of 'no return';

- *Publicity* – criticise the directors' behaviour publicly in the QIP's report; and

- *Disqualification* – recommend action to disqualify them as directors of any company for up to 15 years.

Those owed money – Be firm and prepared to take tough decisions. If you're just nice and fobbed off by excuses, you risk being left badly in the lurch. Don't let the debt pile up or feel you have to carry on dealing with the company at all costs; they may be honest but incapable or over-optimistic, or like many 'out there' may still be playing the old game of robbing Peter to pay Paul, or even themselves. And even if you pursue them later, the chances are that any money recovered is payable into the company and then paid out in due priority to *all* the creditors, not just to you. Prevention here is much better than chasing an uncertain cure.

The contract – Insolvency often triggers a right for the non-insolvent party to end the contract – see #10.4.

CHAPTER 7
Innovation & Technology Issues

7.1 Managing the knowledge business

Every business is a knowledge business, and the main asset of a small business is likely to be in the heads of the people running it. This largely consists of *who they know*, all-important in finding the suppliers or customers necessary to develop the business, and *what they know*. However, what goes around comes around, and every successful business will spawn its own competitors – and potential successors.

> Building a successful business therefore involves both innovating and seeking to protect that innovation appropriately.

This chapter concentrates on identifying how innovation and technology can be legally protected and the next chapter looks at how contracts can help manage risk.

7.2 Intellectual property rights (IPR)

True creativity can involve a substantial investment of time, effort and skill. This resulting product of the intellect, rather than any physical process, is called *intellectual property (IP)*, which is recognised as deserving legal protection. Creators thus acquire *intellectual property rights (IPR)*, manifested in the form of the brand, artistic creation, computer program or invention they protect. Different forms of legal protection then prevent others from copying or making unfair use of that IP in a way likely to detract from the value of the original creative process.

7.3 Can I protect an idea?

Pure ideas – Ideas as such are not protected by law; protection can only arise when the idea is communicated or expressed in some material form, and then only in certain circumstances.

> So if you tell your idea to people at random you'll lose your rights to protect it.

To preserve your rights you need to think about *how and to whom* you communicate your idea. There are two main points to consider here, copyright and confidentiality.

Copyright – Lawyers say that there's *no copyright in an idea*, only in the expression of an idea. This means that to protect your idea you'll have to express it in some form such as writing, recording, film, photography, painting, computer program or the like which will attract copyright protection when made public. However, once the work is communicated publicly, the *idea* behind the work will be 'out in the open', able to be used or copied by others except so far as the idea is expressed so as to achieve its own copyright protection (#7.5). If you write down your idea and post it to yourself, as often advocated, the postmark will support your copyright in *the actual words* and provide evidence of when you had the idea, if there is ever a dispute about that, but it still leaves *the idea* itself open to be copied once communicated.

Confidentiality – Very often new business projects are essentially just ideas which need to be revealed to potential backers or partners but which don't in themselves attract copyright protection.

> The challenge then is to protect the idea by expressing it in some form **without losing protection** in the process of communicating it, be that orally, in writing, in a laptop presentation or any other way. To do this you'll want to ensure that the person receiving the

idea and supporting information is subject to a **duty of confidentiality**.

This might be implicit in the circumstances, such as an obviously private meeting or communication; it might be made explicit ('don't tell anyone because this is confidential'); or it might be preceded by a letter or email stressing the information is confidential. Best of all, before any communication of any key information takes place, is to have a signed *non-disclosure agreement*.

7.4 Non-disclosure agreements (NDAs)

NDAs – Below is a very short form example, which might help if you plan to disclose your idea to someone. It would need appropriate adaptation to the circumstances. It might also be made mutual if the party to whom disclosure is made is also likely to disclose information.

Example: NDA

In consideration of my disclosing to you certain confidential information **(Confidential Information)** concerning a proposed project I have developed relating to *[set out non-confidential outlines]*[1] **(Project)** you agree to treat such information as confidential on the following basis and terms:

1. Confidential Information includes (without limitation) all information in any form (including concepts) that I disclose to you relating to the Project (including any copies of and notes you may make regarding the Project) or relating to *[e.g.* my company, its directors, employees, agents, customers and all others with whom it deals and all financial or trading information, product or marketing plans, proposals, prices or margins].

2. Confidential Information will not include such information as a) has become public knowledge without any breach of this agreement or other breach of confidence on your part or b) you can show that you lawfully held before receiving it from me or c) you are lawfully required to disclose to any regulatory authorities.[2]

3. You will keep the Confidential Information at least as secure as you would keep your own business secrets and will not copy or reproduce it in any form without my prior written consent [except to your directors or professional advisers or other senior employees who have a need to know such information and who are in each case aware of and accept these duties of confidentiality.]

4. You will, automatically if we cease to discuss your potential involvement in the Project or at any time at my request, return to me any Confidential Information in document form and certify in writing that any machine-held Confidential Information has been deleted from all your IT systems.

5. The Confidential Information will remain my exclusive property unless otherwise agreed in writing and its disclosure does not constitute or imply any right to or to use any trade secrets, copyrights or other intellectual property rights within or related to such information.

6. This agreement does not create or imply any joint venture, partnership or business relationship of any kind between us, or any obligation to form such a relationship.

7. Your duties as above will apply for a period of [two/three years] from the date of this agreement.[3]

Signed etc

Notes

[1] *Define what is to be covered* – The project obviously should not be set out in detail in the NDA, as the NDA needs to be signed before the disclosure takes place.

[2] *Authority to disclose to regulatory authorities* – The duty to disclose information to a public authority (such as financial services or competition authorities) will in any case generally override the NDA terms, as will a Freedom of Information Act disclosure requirement when one party has been dealing with a public authority.

[3] *Check there are no other material clauses added* – Some documents called NDAs include broad restrictive covenants (#8.2, 8.3) which have never been discussed and should normally be resisted.

7.5 Copyright

Originality and expression – For something to be protected by copyright it needs to be a) *original* and b) *expressed* in some protectable format. These concepts broadly also apply to most other forms of IP. Copyright is especially important to small businesses because it covers not just written work but also designs, compositions, data (football league tables are protected by copyright) and other plans set out in sufficient detail in an original and coherent way.

Originality – If you just copy the whole of someone else's work, you will infringe their rights; further, since there is no originality in your copy, you'll acquire no rights yourself. If you copy a substantial part of their work, but add something of your own, or copy their work in a different way or medium (such as a photo of a sculpture), you may have originality in your new work such as to claim copyright in that, but your copy may still infringe their copyright.

> So building onto another's work can create real complications unless you have sorted out who owns and can use what results.

Ideas – As seen, ideas are only protected by copyright once they are expressed in some suitable form. Once those ideas are made public, e.g. by publication of the work, copyright will apply to the words but not the ideas except to the extent that the ideas are structured in some substantial original format or sequence. For example, many TV 'format' shows are on the borderline between being just ideas and having a unique format and style sufficient to claim copyright protection. Since copyright is a form of monopoly right, courts will work hard to achieve a sensible balance that protects one person's work without unreasonably stifling another's creativity.

Expression – Writing is just one way of expressing an idea. A literary work (even if thought by others to have no literary merit) acquires protection automatically in most jurisdictions simply by being written down and communicated, although voluntary registration is permitted and has some advantages in a number of countries, such as the USA. Copyright also applies to films/video, recordings (musical and otherwise), photography, artworks and many other formats. The international symbol © is not compulsory in the UK, and does not prove that the work is copyright, but is a useful warning to anyone not to copy without consent.

Joint copyright – Be careful about agreeing joint copyright in certain cases; unless otherwise agreed not only do the proceeds of exploitation need to be split between the joint owners equally but the consent of both (or all) of them needs to be obtained to any use or exploitation of that copyright. If your ex-colleague or (ex-) friend who has joint copyright with you refuses to agree to your proposals you may be stuck. This can become a major issue, especially with jointly developed business plans or software.

Employees and copyright – The general rule here is that, unless otherwise agreed (in writing), copyright in anything devised by an employee in the course of the employee's job belongs to the employer. Some local laws do exceptionally entitle an employee to extra payment for major inventions; otherwise employees can only expect to sell their work on their own account if they can show that work was done in their own time, and preferably with their own facilities, wholly outside their normal job.

Self-employed people – The converse applies here. Unless otherwise agreed the work will belong to the writer, designer or consultant; the customer who has paid for it will merely have an implied licence to use the work for the project in question. So a customer engaging an independent consultant or service provider to write or design something should deal with the copyright position expressly in the engagement contract.

> Frank, a partner in Frank & Co, is instructed to design a novel type of chair for Konrad. Konrad thinks he is getting something unique and is shocked to find Frank designing and selling similar chairs for others or even making them himself. Unless Konrad can show that Frank agreed to assign copyright and/or design rights to him, or that he agreed exclusivity of the design (which will not easily be implied), Konrad will be unable to prevent Frank selling the same design elsewhere.

Infringing the copyright of others – If using someone else's work, be careful that you aren't breaching their copyright. Such a claim can become very costly to deal with, and could also result in your own work having to be withdrawn. There can be confusion as to how much of someone else's work can be copied because the UK 'fair dealing' rules are much tighter than the US 'fair use' exemptions; what might be permitted in the US may be copyright infringement in the UK. In the UK, copying a 'substantial part' is infringement (unless with consent) and may be as little as a paragraph or two of a book or even one or two lines of a famous song or poem. Copying can be verbatim or may be reproduction of enough significant features of another's work, even if the words are different.

Obtaining copyright consent – So it's as well to get written consent (with consideration) if you want to use someone else's copyright, and you'll also need to check that you are dealing with the rightful copyright owner. The original author, artist or designer may not be (or may no longer be) the copyright owner, such as with an employee where the employer may be the first copyright owner, or the copyright might have been assigned. This can partly be covered by enquiry and a suitable warranty (#8.4).

Assignment of copyright – Copyright can be transferred voluntarily by written assignment (note the need for writing here); this is an important option for any small business to bear in mind. If you are designing something you intend to apply generally, ensure you retain the copyright and limit the licence granted to your customers. Conversely, if you are building on someone else's design you'll want to have either have an assignment of their rights in the design or some form of clear written licence as to how and at what cost you can continue to use the design, and what rights you can pass on to others. Without that you risk paying for your own success!

7.6 Other forms of IPR

Many similar concepts apply to other forms of IPR, the following being some of the better known:

- *Patents* – A novel construction or technical process may be registered as a patent. Since novelty is an essential, it's vital no one other than your lawyer or patent agent is given the details before the patent application is published except against a signed NDA (#7.4.). Otherwise there can be no patent.

- *Trademarks* – Most major brands are registered trademarks, designated ® or sometimes RTM, but some remain protected as unregistered marks because of the brand recognition and goodwill they carry. The sign ™ indicates an unregistered mark that is nonetheless regarded as distinctive enough to be protected. Individuals may also have publicity rights in their name which give them broadly similar rights.

- *Database rights* – Copyright can cover data, but where the content is not original but the way in which it is laid out or compiled is, there may be separate legal protection as a database right.

- *Design rights* – Similarly, design rights exist in registered and unregistered form; designs (such as furnishings, clothing and fashion accessories) may also be protected by copyright.

- *Moral rights* – Writers and others producing creative works automatically acquire moral rights which give them the right to be attributed as creators of the work and protect their work from certain kinds of unfair treatment.

- *Know-how* – Copyright will protect against wholesale copying of manuals or computer programs. Otherwise the best approach to protecting business know-how is likely to be through suitable confidentiality provisions as seen above and/or restrictive covenants in employment contracts or contracts for services, covered in the next chapter.

7.7 Privacy and personal information

Expressing ideas and opinions – Before putting your ideas on paper and communicating them, consider whether you might be putting yourself at risk in other ways. One example is libel, defaming some living person in a way to make others think less of them. If it's defamatory and you claim it is true, you must be able to prove it's true, which is rarely easy. Internet chatter or even newspaper reporting is not proof; it may still be untrue. If you claim it is fair comment, it must be expressed not as fact but as opinion in a fair and balanced way, unmotivated by malice.

Privacy – Under the UK and EU human rights legislation, which has broad parallels in the USA and elsewhere, every living person is entitled to respect for their private and family life. The full extent of this right will take time to establish, but it's clear that disclosure of information about someone's private life is only likely to be justified if there is a legitimate issue of public interest to be explored, such as potential abuse by those in positions of authority.

> Business people should therefore think twice, and get advice, before communicating to a third party anything that might infringe the privacy of others.

Personal information (data protection) – Here again, the UK and EU, in common with many other countries, have strong regulations designed to protect personal information held about individuals, not only by the likes of credit card companies and websites, but also by businesses that hold personal data about their customers, third parties or employees. All those may have rights to see (and correct if necessary) personal information held about them and all companies holding personal information have strict duties as to how they may hold and use it, with potential serious liability if it is lost or incorrectly disclosed.

7.8 Technology contracts

Technology contracts have their own distinctive features – Pure hardware sales are governed primarily by sale of goods laws whereas software may be a supply of goods or services, or both – see chapters 4 and 5. For small businesses buying on supplier's terms, as they normally must, the issue may be as much what is *not* in the contract as what is: awareness of some stumbling blocks may make all the difference when things go wrong, as they all too often do. In this area it pays to be detective-like and curious as to what is on offer and what is being promised. Check too that the new system will be compatible with any other systems you rely on and consider what representations and warranties you would want from the supplier (#8.4).

Specification and acceptance testing – The first, and perhaps biggest, challenge may come with the product specification; does this match *both* what the *supplier says* the technology will do *and* what *the customer expects* it to do? A serious mismatch between the two can lead to distress and disputes. Suppliers tend to offer product numbers and technical detail whereas customers want a system that fulfils specified tasks. With major manufacturers producing an ever-changing range of models, there may seem little scope for negotiation here, but assumptions should still be checked and assurances sought before commitment. With bespoke systems a good specification becomes even more important, especially as it is often linked to acceptance tests, setting out the precise functions to be performed and the processing speed required. These are often in turn the triggers for initial, stage and final payments.

Installation and training – If there is reference to alpha or beta testing, it's best to have a definition of what that means, since use can vary and room for argument is usually best avoided. The customer should also consider what support might be required following installation, for how long and the cost implications. Manuals may be provided, physical or electronic, but the customer and its users may need active training to get the best from the new system. These are all issues normally best negotiated from the start.

Software – Software is computer code and is mainly protected by copyright law and, in some limited cases, by patent law. Apart from performance issues, it's important for the customer to appreciate where the software has come from and who has what rights in it.

> The supplier should warrant absolute ownership of the software or disclose its right (or licence) both to use it, develop it (if appropriate) and to licence the customer to use it; the customer will likewise want to know how far its rights go and its ability to licence the software to others (such as its own customers) to use it together with any limitations and/or extra costs on that use.

Support and updates – To keep a new system, especially a bespoke system, in good working order, customers may want to have support pre-agreed, typically by a renewable annual contract. Here are some pointers:

- If support is critical customers should consider a long enough maintenance term (with relative price stability) and whether they can extend it if they wish or cancel if they are dissatisfied.

- This may be linked with a service level agreement defining the detail, for example of response times.

- If buying new software, check that your software licence can be terminated only for your material breach, not just because you want to change the support arrangements. (Otherwise you could be faced with a choice between inadequate support or losing the software you've already paid for.)

- If the system is totally bespoke, could anyone else actually maintain it or sort out any problems? If not, consider what security you might need to ensure you get the support you need.

- Likewise with updates, consider if these are likely to be a normal part of the offering (and, say, available to your competitors). If so, you'll want to build in suitable update – and possibly upgrade – protection.

Exclusivity – Even if you've paid for the development, don't assume that no one else has or will have the same system! (See #4.9 and the Frank and Konrad copyright example in #7.5.) If exclusivity is vital, agree the principles with the developer/supplier and have enough exclusivity written into the contract, even if it is just an exclusive time window, to achieve a head-start in the market whilst preserving the developer's rights in what is effectively its stock-in-trade.

Limitations on use – Many technology products are subject to terms and conditions of use, ranging from a so-called 'click-wrap' *end-user licence agreement (EULA)* for downloads of the latest software, to detailed terms in software development or supply agreements. These typically a) *prevent product misuse* (such as copying or decompiling the software or reproducing the contents of a media product except for a back-up disk or to other media players owned by the licensee) and b) *limit the extent of customer use* (such as to a specified maximum number of users or devices). In the latter case especially it's important for small businesses to check early on and build in the capacity for growth, e.g. by having the contract specify reasonable extra payment for potential additional users in the future.

Liability and force majeure – Computer contracts can be plagued by disclaimers and limitations of liability, so look at the next chapter (8) before you negotiate your technology contract. Similarly consider force majeure in chapter 9 as to what might happen if unexpected events occur.

Source code – This is the human-readable version of the software. If you have bespoke software and the developer/supplier becomes insolvent, you'll need to use someone else to help, and they will need the source code. Look at escrow arrangements via organisations such as NCC Group, and consider whether they should extend to the developer's breach and no-fault termination as well as developer's insolvency.

7.9 Some examples

The following hypothetical examples show some of the principles mentioned above at work, considering in turn a) the type of knowledge, b) where it came from and c) what duties arise in relation to it.

- *The freelance writer (Sam – see chapter 6) – Sam hopefully writes his articles and his book from original sources and without infringing anyone else's copyright or libelling them or breaching their privacy (#7.7).* Analysis: Sam will acquire copyright in his work by virtue of writing it as a freelance. His magazine and book publishers will take licences to publish the relevant work, probably both exclusive licenses but the magazine publishers having a relatively short period of exclusivity whereas the book publishers will probably require exclusivity for the full term of copyright (70 years from the end of the year of Sam's death) provided the book continues to sell through.

- *The student – Mark has just left college and wants to start his own business selling a revolutionary measuring device via the internet. He developed the idea as a research project with some help from his college and is buying a list of potential internet customers to help him get started.* Analysis: a) The knowledge here is in the device Mark has designed; b) Mark was a student and had help from his college (and possibly colleagues) so he needs to be clear what rights he and they have in this invention (some institutions have sole or part-ownership of any IPR in return for the facilities and training they provide); c) if Mark has joint rights in the device he would need to agree with the college (and/or his colleagues) a basis for exploiting the design and how costs and revenue would be shared. As to the customer list, Mark would need to buy the right to use the information as he wished, being aware of the data protection rights of the customers and checking that the sellers of the list had acquired the rights to process and pass on that personal data to third parties.

- *The geek – Louise is an experienced computer programmer, who has devised a template application. She wants to use this to provide bespoke products for the growing app market.* Analysis: a) The type of knowledge here is computer software, protectable primarily by copyright; b) Louise is free to use her general skill and experience as a programmer subject to two main considerations – (1) that she is not under any confidentiality (#7.4) or non-compete (#8.3) obligations to any previous employer, client or other third party and (2) that she is not using anyone's else's copyright or other IPR without their consent; c) If her template includes third party software she needs to know that this software is open source (which would limit any future exclusivity available to her template) or its use is permitted by the relevant third party user licence, not just for her but for any licensee of hers using an app including the third party content, or she will need express consent.

- *The campaigner – After some years of experience with a pharmaceutical company, Susan, a keen campaigner for the third world, has discovered that she can source much needed medicines from a reputable producer prepared to white label its products for distinct overseas markets. She is planning to sell these direct into deprived areas.* Analysis: Susan has good intentions but will know that the pharmaceutical world is highly protective of its brand names and huge product development investment. There are branding issues here (and the pharma company might choose to white-label its products to seek to avoid any brand damage if things went wrong). Otherwise Susan's knowledge base (a) is both technical in terms of the products themselves and also market-related, (b) arising in each case largely from the one company. Her duties (c) in this scenario are not just to that company but significantly to any users of the medicines for possible personal injury or even death in using them, risks that normally cannot be excluded by law. This would be a challenging venture with the risk of personal liability in contract, in negligence (#9.4) and under the product safety laws of other countries. Susan, rather than taking personal liability, should think about securing the protection of a limited liability company and also seeking a solid indemnity from her producer and/or distributor.

- *The market researcher – Clive has worked in market research for many years, learning the business in general and also building up many good contacts. He now plans to go it alone, starting with two clients from his old employer.* Analysis: To what extent will Clive be using information derived from previous employers? As already seen, the law will not prevent him using his general skill and experience, but may intervene if, for example, Clive intends to use blueprints, training materials or customer lists (all written materials protected by copyright) taken from his previous employers. The start point is to consider his contracts (of employment or for services) with his previous employers or clients (especially recent ones), whether any materials might be their property and whether there are any current restrictive covenants. Clive should then consider if and to what extent he can use these materials or, assuming he would not get consent from his previous employees (now competitors), to what extent he should start again, using his own experience and knowledge of the business rather than risk a claim from his former employers or clients, which could bring his business to a sudden halt.

CHAPTER 8
Contracts & Risk

8.1 Introduction

Risk, benefit and cost – Imagine someone says that they'll sell you their car for a stated price but they can't guarantee either that it's theirs to sell or that it will work. You probably wouldn't want the car at all or, if you did agree to take the risks, you'd expect to pay a great deal less. This assumes you were even told about the reservations; if you weren't told, you'd certainly expect some redress if things did go wrong. This chapter considers how you might think about and plan ahead for likely risks and, if things do go wrong, be clear who picks up the pieces – and the bill.

Negotiating risk allocation – Once you've identified the more likely risks, you'll then need to think how best to deal with them in the contract, for instance by trying to draw out the other party's commitments in clear obligations and the underlying assumptions by warranties, covering the risk of 'left-field' claims by indemnities, and seeking to limit the consequences of your own (unintended) failure by a suitable exclusion and limitation clause. These approaches are explained below.

Which risks?

> Things need to be kept in perspective when managing risk; you can't cover all possible eventualities, so it's best to concentrate on the more likely possibilities plus risks which may be less likely but where the damage could be bigger.

Many concerns for large companies, such as environmental issues, reputational damage and breach of competition law, are probably less likely or less serious for the small business, but the loss of a single major contract or customer could hit the start-up operation hard. Worse still may be a protracted lawsuit, especially if a little advance planning could have avoided it.

8.2 Restricting the other party

The relevance of restrictions – Part of risk planning is being clear at the outset what the products or service supplied can or cannot be used for. In consumer sales this links to the need for appropriate instructions and warnings – see 'liability for product safety' in #4.10. In business deals, you might want to think about two main ways in which you'd want to restrict the other party, one being a *limitation on the rights granted*, such as limiting the number of permitted users of a software programme, and the other being *an obligation on them not to do something*, such as not to use your own know-how to compete with you. As a rule, it's easier to enforce, and thus better drafting, to define the rights narrowly rather than give broad rights and then a series of prohibitions on the licensee. The same principle applies with exclusion clauses, as seen below.

Personal and business know-how – The law distinguishes the general skill and knowledge that someone develops in the course of their work (*personal know-how*) from their knowledge of confidential information about the specific business they serve (*business secrets*) – see the Clive example in #7.9.

> As a general rule it's difficult to restrict use of personal know-how, because people are entitled to use the general skills they've learned doing their job. Business secrets, on the other hand, can be protected to the extent a) they represent a real asset of that business and b) the restrictions go only so far as reasonably necessary to protect that business.

Negotiating restrictions – Negotiating restrictions on someone's behaviour is an area which even experienced businesspeople can find challenging. Here are some suggestions to reduce the pain:

- *Timing* – Raise the issue early on.

- *Openness* – Be clear that your concerns are generic business ones and not personal.

- *Mutuality* – Be prepared to offer suitable restrictions yourself if appropriate.

- *Reasonableness* – Keep the restrictions proportionate to the services being provided and the risk involved.

- *Writing it down* – Ensure the contract reflects these principles from the outset.

8.3 Non-compete clauses (restrictive covenants)

The principles – This is a complex legal area, with laws varying across the world, but here are some guidelines:

- *Extent* – Limit the clause to the *type of goods and/or services* being dealt with under the contract.

- *Scope* – Limit the clause to *the people with whom the service provider is actually likely to be dealing,* e.g. those involved in dealing direct with your product or customers at senior levels. Include agents and representatives, but don't cast the net too wide, for example by including worldwide associated companies in unrelated businesses.

- *Area* – Limit the clause to activities or customers based in the *identifiable geographical area and distinct product market* most at risk.

- *Time* – Always limit the clause *in time*, and go for the minimum period reasonably necessary for essential protection. Restrictions should not normally exceed the term of the agreement plus six or, at most, 12 months. For any large businesses (to limit competition law prohibitions), the overall period should not exceed the term of the agreement up to five years plus one year afterwards.

Non-compete/non-dealing/non-solicitation – Your customers may know if a former employee of yours has approached them for business, but they won't want to get caught up in a dispute, so you'll ideally not want to rely on their evidence. Consider:

- *A non-solicitation clause* – prohibiting one party from approaching the other's customers for competing business (harder to prove – see above – but easier to enforce legally if proved);

- *A non-dealing clause* – prohibiting one party from dealing with the other party's customers in relation to specific products in a specific area (see scope above);

- *A non-compete clause* – prohibiting involvement in a competing business in a specific area (thus more restrictive and correspondingly harder to enforce).

An example – The clause below is given with a heavy health warning. Its enforceability is not guaranteed! It is just an example of applying the principles in this chapter, needing careful adaptation to the circumstances. It assumes the capitalised words are defined terms, *Customer* being the company for whom the *Supplier* is working, *Client* a client of the *Customer*, *Services* the services covered by the agreement itself and *Market* the relevant product market. The three sub-clauses follow the three types of restriction referred to in the previous paragraph. Note that the non-compete provision in c) is only likely to be enforceable if Services and Market are narrowly defined and Supplier is not prevented from using general personal know-how and experience in that market overall. The clause should not be used to block fair competition.

Supplier recognises the confidentiality of the Customer's relationships with its Clients and its knowledge of the Market. Accordingly Supplier undertakes with Customer that Supplier will not during the Term [and for a period of six/twelve months after Termination] in competition with the Customer:

(a) approach any Client or solicit the business of any Client by offering or agreeing to provide services [in the Market] of the same kind as the Services supplied by the Customer to that Client; or

(b) deal with or provide services [in the Market] to any Client of the same kind as the Services; or

(c) be engaged, involved or interested in any business providing services [in the Market]of the same kind as the Services *[specify a limited geographical area as well as a narrow product market if possible]*.

8.4 Warranties and Indemnities

Negotiating warranties and indemnities – Seeking warranties is a form of comfort and an important part of risk planning for both parties, but can easily become another emotive area to negotiate. Once again good sense and a fair balance can help, treating warranties as a form of reminder or checklist (for both parties) of important issues to avoid later problems and indemnities as cover against third party risks.

- *Assumptions* – What are you assuming about the other party? – e.g. that they are qualified and experienced in the type of work you want them to carry out or, with a rights deal, that they own the rights being offered and there are no disputes relating to them. If the assumptions are important to you, propose warranties to confirm them. If this produces a disclosure of something you didn't know and you choose to go ahead anyway, you'll understand the risks better; if the disclosure really disturbs you, you can still withdraw. If the warranty is given in the contract and proves false, you'll have a claim for damages for your loss.

- *Listening* – Listen carefully to how the other party answers your questions, both for content and manner. Question and test where appropriate; what would make you change your mind if you had known about it? Make a note of any key statements, positive or negative, and be ready to bring these back 'to the table' at the appropriate time, as warranties, indemnities or other contract terms.

- *Mutuality* – If you are requesting warranties, be prepared to offer suitable warranties yourself.

Example – a basic short form warranty and indemnity from a software development agreement

Supplier warrants to Customer that a) Supplier owns [and/or] has the authority to grant the rights set out in this agreement without the need for any third party consents and b) provision of the Services and Deliverables under this agreement will not infringe the Intellectual Property Rights or otherwise breach any legal rights of any third party[1]. Supplier will give all reasonable assistance to and indemnify Customer against any losses, damages or costs suffered or incurred by Customer[2] in relation to any third party claim against Customer arising from breach or alleged breach[3] of this warranty[4] (**Claim**) provided first that Customer notifies Supplier as soon as practicable on becoming aware of the Claim and keeps Supplier fully informed on any issues material to the Claim and second that the Supplier has exclusive handling of the Claim in conjunction with its professional advisers. Neither party will unreasonably refuse its consent to a settlement recommended by the Supplier's legal advisers[5].

Notes

[1] The warranty aims to reassure the customer that the supplier (or software developer) is not using third party software that might cause a claim against the customer.

[2] This is the basic indemnity wording.

[3] The indemnity here actually covers both actual warranty breaches and *alleged* breaches. The customer may get cover against third party claims, but this wording also leaves the supplier vulnerable to defending *unjustified* claims.

[4] There are well-established rules to assess damages for breach of contract. Because indemnities can mean paying more, many lawyers seek to limit indemnities (as here) to breaches of warranty, not just any breach of contract.

[5] The indemnity also contains a *claims-handling* provision. There are many potential issues in such clauses but this short-form provision covers the basics of requiring the customer to keep the supplier informed of relevant issues relating to the claim, whilst preventing either party from blocking a possible favourable settlement.

8.5 Exclusion and Limitation Clauses

What then happens if one party does break the contract? A breach of contract will usually entitle the 'innocent party' (*victim*) to claim compensation (*damages*) from the party at fault (*defaulter*); a very serious breach (*material breach*) might give rights to terminate. See also #9.9 on breach and damages. The liability for damages may in turn be covered by an exemption clause in the contract, a vital part of risk management. There are broadly two types:

- *exclusion clauses*, which seek to *exclude all liability* for the type of loss in question;

- *limitation clauses*, which seek to *limit ('cap') liability* for either specified or overall loss.

Damages

> Damages are normally based on the value of the benefits that the victim was entitled to under the contract, but did not receive because of the breach.

With goods, that entitlement may include the cost of repair or replacement, plus any higher costs of buying the goods from elsewhere. With services it may cover the cost of making good any errors of the defaulter and/or of hiring someone else to finish off the work.

Direct and foreseeable loss – How far then does this obligation to pay damages go? What happens if something unexpected occurs? What if the victim loses the contract because of the defaulter's failure and then loses a long-term customer as a consequence of losing the contract? Laws of different countries vary somewhat here but the English law principles set down in the 1850s still hold good in many countries. The rule is that damages will reflect two kinds of loss; the first is loss which flows *naturally* from the breach (in the ordinary course of things) without any intervening cause (known as '*direct loss*'), for which suppliers will generally be liable; the second is loss that arises *indirectly* from the breach but in a way that might reasonably have been foreseen ('*foreseeable loss*'). Suppliers will be liable for this indirect but foreseeable loss only if *at the time the contract was made* the supplier knew, or could reasonably foresee, the customer's special circumstances. Hindsight is not applicable here!

Consequential loss – This term causes confusion; it does not mean 'foreseeable'. UK courts tend to interpret it (following the original 1850s judgement) as meaning the type of loss that was *not* reasonably foreseeable by the parties *as a consequence* of the breach. The result is that many clauses that seek to exclude liability for consequential loss do not in fact exclude loss which was indirect but was still foreseeable (as above).

Legislation limiting exemption clauses – The use of exemption clauses may be limited by law, quite strictly in consumer contracts, and also in B2B contracts. For example, the English *Unfair Contract Terms Act* applies where one party (seller or buyer) trades under its 'standard' terms of business and the exemption goes too far. The relative bargaining position of the parties, any alternatives offered and the availability of insurance are all factors considered in assessing what is reasonable and what is too far.

How best to handle the issue? – Whether you want an exemption clause depends on which side of the fence you are on. Suppliers generally want maximum exemption and customers generally want the supplier to be fully liable. If, however, both parties have material obligations (other than payment), then both may want such a clause. The key is to find a sensible balance, but unfortunately case reports are full of examples where the parties, having agreed everything else, have fallen out over the exemption clause. So deal with this early on. Bear in mind too that any uncertainty in the drafting will be interpreted against the party seeking to rely on the limitation.

Here is one approach:

- as a prelude, consider what risks you can reasonably foresee;

- define in the contract which party takes which risks and to what extent; and

- consider who is best placed to insure each risk (see below); then, subject to insurance:

- exclude liability for indirect and/or consequential loss[1];

- limit liability for direct and any other forms of loss not specifically excluded[2];

- add an entire agreement and non-reliance clause[3];

- state that the exemption does not apply to a) any death or personal injury caused through the party's negligence or b) fraud or fraudulent misrepresentation of the party (or its employees)[4]; and

- balance the exemptions against the length of the contract term and the force majeure clause (#9.6).

Notes

[1] Unless there is a specific foreseeable loss which the parties agree should be covered.

[2] The trick is to find an amount that is enough both to give real incentive for the supplier to perform and reasonable redress to the customer, without crippling the supplier if things go wrong. This may be linked to a multiple of the price of the goods or services, or earnings over a suitable period.

[3] These clauses seek to exclude liability for prior agreements or pre-contract representations (#9.5).

[4] An attempted exclusion of such risks is likely to be unenforceable and may be illegal.

Loss of profits – A common problem area is loss of profits. Such claims can be very substantial if there are knock-on effects, with difficult questions arising as to what really caused each loss, so this can become a major issue. Bear in mind that it's often impossible for the supplier to insure against the customer's loss; the customer itself may be better placed to insure (#8.6) against loss of profits/additional cost of working, at least to a degree. One approach therefore is to limit loss of profits claims to direct and immediate loss affecting current contracts only, excluding loss of future profits. This may leave open the difficult issue of claims for loss of goodwill or payments the customer may have to make to its own customers to keep them loyal.

Sole remedy clauses – Sole remedy clauses (see the example at #5.10) state that the only remedy an innocent party can have for a specified breach is the remedy stated in the contract, typically the replacement of defective goods or the return of a deposit. This would then preclude any claim for any other loss, such as immediate loss of profits directly resulting (see above) from the defaulter's failure to perform. This is another, and more subtle, form of limitation clause to look out for.

8.6 Insurance

Insurance is a key part of risk management, and contract parties should review their insurance cover (and policy terms) when negotiating relevant contracts. For example, consider what financial loss might be caused by a breakdown of equipment. A customer will expect to look to the supplier to get the equipment going again or replace it if it is seriously defective. The supplier will probably have some form of cover for replacement costs for the equipment, but the customer can probably more easily insure against the loss of data, loss of profits and any additional costs of working in the meantime arising from the breakdown.

> The customer may be better relying on its own loss of profits cover than battling over the exemption clause on that issue.

However, insurers normally have the *right of subrogation* under the policy, which means that if the insurers pay out under the customer's policy, they can stand in the customer's shoes to pursue whatever legal remedies the customer has against the supplier under the contract. All the more reason for suppliers to want to limit their liability!

8.7 Competition Law

Exclusivity arrangements (#4.9) or restrictive covenants (#8.3) may restrict trade, and competition law seeks to prevent businesses making arrangements that limit 'healthy' competition in their market, whether that is the aim or just the result of their actions. Similar regimes operate in the USA, UK, the rest of the European Union and many other areas. There are fines and other potentially draconian sanctions for breach. Fortunately for small businesses there are several thresholds below which businesses are deemed unlikely to be affecting the market, but defining what 'the market' is can be problematic. Most small businesses will be well within these threshold levels, but if you are in a narrow market and your share is 10% or more (or in some cases as little as 5%) you should take further advice. If it is approaching 30% or more you need to take special care. In any case you should beware any so-called '*hardcore restrictions*', even if your market share is small. Specifically:

- *Don't agree to fixed resale prices* – Whilst you can recommend a retail price (RRP) for your products you can't insist that your customer resells at a given or minimum price (except with '*true agency*' as below).

- *Beware limiting production or technical developments.*

- *Don't share business secrets* with your competitors.

- Beware enforcing or agreeing *territorial restrictions* as to resales.

Active, passive and internet sales – The European Union, like the US, has a single internal market, so that products available in any member state should be available to customers in any other member state from the same supplier on equivalent terms. There are some limited exceptions to this, such as specialised reseller distribution networks. Also *active sales* (where the consumer is targeted by the retailer) into another territory may be lawfully restricted, whereas *passive sales* (where the consumer takes the initiative) generally cannot be prevented. For this purpose the internet is regarded as a passive medium, so that, unless there is clear evidence of a consumer in another territory being specifically targeted, internet etailers cannot be prevented from supplying across state boundaries within the overall market if the customer takes the initiative.

True agency agreements – Competition law bites when there are two or more independent companies involved. Since an agent is seen as an extension of its principal, it is not treated as independent – provided the agent is a *true agent* (#4.2). If there is a true agency, the principal can fix the resale prices of the products sold by the agent on its behalf. But take care, as getting this wrong can mean infringing competition law.

8.8 Negligence

Legal liability may arise outside the contract if someone is injured by the negligence of another. This is the basis of claims for personal injury, such as medical claims or injury/car damage caused by another's careless driving. The same principle can apply if damage or injury is caused by faulty goods or negligent actions. To claim you'd need to show that the other person owed you a duty of care, was in breach of that duty and that you suffered loss or damage as a result. There doesn't therefore have to be a contract for such claims to arise, and indeed where there is a contract and injury or damage occurs, there may be alternative claims in negligence and contract.

8.9 The need for legal advice

There are comments in the introduction and elsewhere in this book about the need for legal advice, and here is a case in point. The management of contract risk is highly complex, with the law constantly developing and the financial consequences potentially major, so you are highly recommended to seek advice from a lawyer experienced in such contractual issues, which is a specialist subject even for lawyers. This chapter should then give you a good background and briefing to help you get effective professional support at a sensible cost.

CHAPTER 9
Living with Contracts

9.1 Contracts as working documents

Events – Contracts may be signed speedily or only after months of wrangling; in either case the tendency is to breathe a sigh of relief, put the contract in a drawer and forget about it. This assumes that the parties will remember all the contract terms, that all goes to plan and that life stays the same. The evidence, however, is all to the contrary. Imperfect understandings, faulty recollections and changing times all suggest that contracts should be kept under regular review.

> All manner of events can and do occur, some of which may be beneficial and others of which can add to costs or reduce if not actually negate the benefit expected from the contract.

These events may be external and beyond the control of the parties, but many are just down to oversight or failure to act when it matters. Here are just *some* examples:

- *Supply* – The supplier, pre-occupied elsewhere, does the wrong thing or the right thing at the wrong time.

- *Payment* – The customer doesn't check the contract and fails to pay on time.

- *Notices* – A party serves a notice on the other which turns out to be invalid.

- *Breach* – One party breaks the contract but the other takes no action or itself breaches the contract.

Changing the contract – If there is an *agreed change*, ensure this is properly documented (including extra 'consideration' – #1.4) and signed. By the same token, be careful you don't *inadvertently* change things or agree to unintended changes, which can easily happen. One party doing something different from what the contract says, and the other accepting the change (expressly or by being aware and doing nothing), may be treated as an agreed contract variation, especially if there is no going back to the original position. (See also 'acquiescence' in #9.3 below.)

> So if the other party acts differently from the contract terms, decide promptly whether you agree with the change or let them know you require them to do what they promised to do. Delay may endanger your legal position.

9.2 Transfer and assignment

Assignment – An 'assignment' is a transfer of non-physical property, such as a contract or licence. Most contracts can be assigned without the other party's consent, unless a) the contract prohibits this or b) the personal identity of the parties is critical to the deal (such as artist and client, author and publisher or musician and record company). Is the identity of the other party critical to you? If it is or may be, seek an express prohibition against assignment. If you need to get consent, make sure you get it in writing, since an assignment which is neither permitted nor agreed is an irremediable breach (see chapter 10).

A sample assignment clause

Assignment: Neither party may assign or transfer its rights or obligations under this agreement without the prior written consent of the other party[1] [, such consent not to be unreasonably withheld or delayed].[2] [This clause will not prevent the assignment or transfer of rights or obligations to an Associated Company.][3] Subject to the above, this agreement is binding upon each party's successors and assigns and personal representatives, as the case may be.[4]

Notes

[1] See above.

[2] The optional wording gives some control in longer contracts, where much can change.

[3] See below under groups of companies.

[4] The final sentence is really a reminder that the benefit and burden of contracts pass (generally together) to any assignee or, in the case of death of an individual, their estate as represented by their official personal representatives.

Ongoing liability, release and novation – It's not possible to assign the obligations ('burden') under a contract without the benefits. In any event assigning a contract does not relieve the original parties of their obligations. Accordingly, if you can and do assign a contract, even with consent, always get the *assignee* (the person to whom you assign it) to undertake to perform all your obligations under the contract from the assignment date. Nevertheless, if they fail to do so, the other original party can come back to you.

> Paul has a contract with Bill which Paul wants to assign to Steve so that Paul is 'off the hook'. To achieve this he'll need either a) an assignment to Steve with consent and an express release from Bill or b) a novation, signed by Paul and Steve as well as Bill. A novation is a new contract where Paul is expressly released from the original agreement by Bill, leaving Bill and Steve as the only new contract parties. Unless Paul is paying Bill for the release, the agreement should be signed as a deed.

Sub-contracting and sub-licensing – Sub-contracting is delegation of all or part of your role whilst retaining full responsibility (such as using sub-contractors in the construction industry); a sub-licence is a form of sub-contract of intellectual property or similar rights, such as copyright or software rights. Always check to see if sub-contracting is restricted by the contract, or if permitted, what terms apply.

Groups of companies – Companies which are part of larger groups will often want to be able to assign to other members of the same group (see the optional wording under assignment above), which is normally acceptable. A small business may be more concerned to secure (or may be asked for) a *change of control clause* permitting one party to terminate if the other party is taken over (#10.6).

9.3 'Boilerplate' clauses

Longer form contracts typically include so-called *boilerplate clauses*, often regarded as 'the small print', but having potentially significant implications. The next sections give some typical examples and why they may matter.

9.4 Notices

The notices clause is designed to ensure there is an agreed way to serve any notices required under the contract. Always check this provision when serving (or receiving) a notice and follow it strictly, as failure to comply with all requirements may make your notice ineffective. Here's an example:

> *Notices:* Any notice or other communication under this agreement[1] a) must be in writing delivered personally[2] or sent by [first class post][3], [or sent by email with a delivery receipt[4],] to the relevant party's address as below or as last notified to the other[5]; b) is deemed to have been given[6] on the day it is delivered personally, or on the second day following the date it was sent by [first class] post [or on the next working day following transmission by email][7].

Notes

[1] If you're not sure what needs 'notification' it's probably best to err on the side of caution.

[2] Personal delivery is best backed-up with a letter or email – or at the minimum a diary note.

[3] This may need adaptation. For example, some countries require pre-paid registered delivery.

[4] Many companies still dislike notices sent by email, preferring fax with clearer evidence of transmission and receipt. But not all businesses have fax, or others have a half-defunct machine in a corner that no one looks at. So this needs careful thinking about. If email is used, reference to a delivery receipt may help, but it's not infallible. With breach/termination notices it may be worth insisting on personal delivery or post plus email, as time may be critical.

[5] Worth including but remember to notify any changed delivery or email address.

[6] The date notice is deemed to be given may be key for some notices.

[7] Some contracts define 'Business Day', normally excluding weekends and state holidays.

9.5 Entire agreement

Suppliers' assurances about the quality or performance of their products don't always find their way into the supply contract! If the statement proves false customers may claim it induced them to sign the contract, leading to a *misrepresentation claim*, sometimes also used to justify non-payment. To counteract this suppliers have developed the *entire agreement clause*, which states that the contract contains all the agreed terms to the exclusion of anything else. To this has been added a clause stating that the customer (or other party) has not relied on any pre-contract statement, even if one was made (and even if the customer did rely on it!) Here's an example, and small businesses should take heed of note 3 especially.

> *Entire agreement and non-reliance:* This agreement [and any documents referred to in it][1] constitute(s) the entire agreement between the parties, and supersede(s) all other agreements or arrangements between the parties (whether written or oral, express or implied), relating to the subject matter of this agreement[2]. Each party accepts that it is relying entirely on the terms set out in this agreement and not on any pre-contract statement, representation or misrepresentation made by or on behalf of the other party except to the extent (if at all) specifically set out in this agreement[3].

Notes

[1] Include the extra wording if there is more than one document.

[2] This covers a wide range of possible issues. The customer should check that all the supplier's 'promises' are set out in the contract; otherwise the customer may have no redress even if able to prove they were made.

[3] Customers should not be shy about insisting that such statements are spelled out in the contract. If not, especially with such a clause included, the customer can place little reliance on them.

9.6 Force majeure

This phrase is now generally used in place of 'Act of God', but the concept is the same. The aim is to say that it won't be a breach if a party cannot perform on time or at all due to events outside their control. The issue may be whether the event is indeed outside their control rather than something they could have avoided with some forethought. The clause may also give the chance to exit the contract if the resultant delay is likely to affect either party badly.

> A force majeure clause can be worthwhile for both supplier and customer, but should not be a get-out for failure to pay, poor equipment maintenance or bad staff relations.

Some clauses set out force majeure examples in detail; the example below leaves it open as to what is actually beyond someone's reasonable control, adding an obligation to notify, to help plan in good time and rights to terminate, which should be considered according to individual circumstances. Note that adverse economic times are unlikely to be accepted as force majeure!

> *Force majeure:* Neither party will be liable for any failure to perform or delay in performing any obligation under this agreement, other than an obligation to make any payment, for circumstances beyond its reasonable control provided that it promptly notifies the other party of such circumstances and uses its reasonable endeavours to mitigate their effects. If such circumstances [are likely to] continue to prevent substantial performance of this agreement for more than [60 days], either party may terminate this agreement on [30] days' written notice to the other.

9.7 Choice of law and jurisdiction

Choice of law and courts – This clause can be useful if the contract has any international element. Mandatory laws of one country may overrule the contract but it's worth the parties considering not only which country's law applies but also which country's courts will hear the case, which is not just a matter of practical convenience but may also affect the attitude of the local judge. A supplier probably wants to have its home law apply, which also ties into its supply arrangements, whereas retailers need to comply with consumer law at point of sale, so there may be a tug of war here. Small businesses will generally want their local law to apply, but will not always succeed. They may be exposed to product safety laws (#4.10) wherever their products are ultimately sold, but should where possible seek to limit their contractual responsibilities to areas where they have operational control.

> *Law and jurisdiction:* This agreement will be governed and construed in accordance with the laws of [England and Wales] and the parties submit to the exclusive jurisdiction of the [English] courts.

9.8 Some other boilerplate clauses

Severance clause – This clause, less likely to affect small businesses, aims to prevent the whole contract failing just because specific clauses are excessive, such as being unfairly restrictive or breaching competition law.

> *Severability:* Any provision of this agreement which is held to be illegal or unenforceable will, to the extent necessary, be omitted from this agreement. The enforceability of the remainder will not be affected.

Acquiescence – Failure to insist on your legal rights under a contract may be treated as accepting any breach and/or waiving your rights, preventing you from enforcing them in the future. A non-waiver clause may be help whilst you are considering or negotiating what to do, but should not be regarded as a complete panacea.

> *Waivers:* Neither party will be affected by any delay or failure in exercising or any partial exercising of its rights under this agreement unless it has signed an express written waiver or release.

Changes to the agreement – Similarly, to reduce (but not eliminate) the risk of being deemed to have accepted a change in the terms of the contract by your actions (see 9.1), a no-variation clause may help.

Variations: No variations of this agreement are effective unless made in writing signed by the parties or their authorised agents.

Third party rights – Sometimes you don't have to be a party to a contract to claim rights under it. Imagine that Smith has a contract to sell to Jones on the basis that Jones pays Green (perhaps in settlement of a debt Smith owes Green). Green may not be a party to the contract, but may still be able to claim payment off Jones (if Smith fails to do so), provided Green's stake in the contract gives him a 'beneficial interest' in the proceeds. The following sort of clause is often added to make it clear where *no* such arrangement is intended.

Right of third parties: The parties intend that no term of this agreement may be enforced by any person who is not a party to it.

9.9 Breach, Damages and Enforcement

Contracts are broken all the time, most breaches causing no real damage and being easily remedied whilst a spirit of cooperation exists between the parties. Bigger problems tend to arise when there is a) a more major failure to pay; b) serious delivery or performance failure; c) a change in the people you are dealing with or their commitment to the project; or d) external events, such as financial crises, embargos or shortage of materials.

> Before you respond, keep calm and try to find out what's happening; if you are the one at fault, it's often best to explain why and what you can do, provided you then do it. But if the relationship has started to go wrong, or if either party is seeking an excuse to pressurise the other, even small issues can escalate into something much bigger.

Always look at the contract carefully before you go any further, and seek early professional advice; it's very easy to make a mistake at this point. Here are some guidelines and some options:

- *Breach of contract* – A breach arises when one party does not comply with the contract, either by inaction (not doing what is required) or action prohibited by the contract.

- *Liability for damages* – Breach may trigger a damages claim if it causes loss to the other party, either under a specific term of the contract (such as liquidated damages) or under the general law (#9.10).

- *Remedying the breach* – If you can remedy the breach, i.e. put the mistake right, there may be no loss and thus no claim. If there is some loss, generally the earlier the remedy, the less the loss is likely to be.

- *Notice to remedy* – Most contracts don't require notice to be given of a breach except as a possible prelude to termination, so don't wait for notice but remedy as soon as you can.

- *Admissions* – Initially try to avoid admitting a breach or liability and concentrate on possible remedies. Try also to keep good relations with the other party through this and not be seen as too clever or evasive.

- *Settling claims* – If you try to negotiate a settlement, ensure that your discussions are *without prejudice*. So long as you are genuinely negotiating to settle a dispute, this phrase should prevent any offer being used against you if the case goes to court. You should also make any specific proposals *subject to contract* (#2.2) until you are ready to reach agreement.

- *Repudiation* – Take notice of the contract and keep to it; otherwise you too will be in breach. Don't do or say anything like: 'I don't care what the contract says, I'm going to do …!' as this could amount to *repudiation* of the contract, effectively denying its validity or application to you. This would shift the onus and give the other party the right to terminate against you – and claim full damages for *your breach*. Again, get early legal advice here as mistakes are easily made and can be very costly.

- *Payment failure* – see chapter 6.

- *Mitigation of loss* – Contract victims must take reasonable action to reduce their loss, e.g. by seeking another supplier or other customers for what cannot be provided or paid for. Their claim should then be for the difference between the contract price and what they had to pay (or receive from) someone else for what had been promised under the contract.

- *Liquidated damages* – Where the extent of loss, and thus damages, may be uncertain, some contracts provide for a specific amount (called 'liquidated') to be paid in compensation (damages) for certain breaches. This can be useful, but only if the amount is a genuine pre-estimate of the loss or a fairly agreed sum which can, if necessary, be justified to a court. If it's just a penalty to deter breach, unrelated to likely loss, it will be unenforceable unless it has a strong commercial justification.

- *Arbitration or mediation* – If there is a real dispute, don't get righteous. Remember there are normally arguments both ways. There may be an industry body or dispute resolution forum that can help. Note that arbitration is normally binding and mediation non-binding; unless the contract provides for this both parties would have to agree to either route.

- *Serious breaches* – If a breach is serious enough (*material breach*), it might justify termination by the other party. Termination is examined in the next chapter. If the contract is terminated for breach, the victim will be able to recover for the total loss of the rest of the contract value, as well as their immediate loss, so the stakes can be high.

CHAPTER 10
Ending Contracts

10.1 How contracts end

General principles – Contracts come to an end for various reasons. One is that the period – or *term* – of the contract expires and is not renewed. Or one party may exercise a right in the contract to terminate it early, either for any reason (*without cause*) or with cause as set out in the contract, for example if there is a material breach or insolvency. This chapter looks at the various ways contracts may end and the implications arising.

The contract term – When planning a contract you should consider how long you want the contract to last and how it can be ended. If not, you might:

- become trapped in the contract long after you wanted; or

- lose the contract just as the real benefits are coming through; or

- fail to end the contract properly or at the best time.

Where do I find the 'term'?

- Check the *definitions* section (if there is one) to see if it's defined there, e.g. under 'Term'. This may cross-refer to other definitions such as 'Commencement Date' (see example below).

- Look for a *clause* setting out how long the contract lasts, like the one below.

- Then look at the *termination clauses*, both with and without cause.

- Finally, look for *any other clauses* where one or other party has the right to terminate.

- Then it's a good idea to note any critical date(s) by which notice must be given or other action taken.

An example – The example below is fairly basic. This specifies a Commencement Date, which is normally clearer than simply having the contract start from the date of the agreement, which may remain uncertain until the last moment.

> *Defined term* – Commencement Date *[insert date agreement provisions are due to start]*
>
> *Operative clause* – Term – This agreement starts on the Commencement Date and, unless terminated earlier in accordance with its terms, will end on *[specify* date].

10.2 How long should the term be?

The principles – Apart from one-off sales of goods, business contracts can vary in length from a few months to many years. Generally longer periods breed more conditions, since prices, the value of money and other circumstances can change substantially over time.

> Shorter terms (two years or less) usually mean simpler contracts, leading to a speedier conclusion. Longer periods tend to introduce more variables and more complexity, so if you want a signed contract quickly, it's worth keeping things shorter and simpler first time round.

What happens once the term has expired? – You'll also need to be clear what happens after the initial specified term ends. It depends on the precise wording; typically the contract will:

(a) *end (or expire) automatically,* if there is no renewal language; this is simple but runs the risk of having no clear contract in place if the parties just carry on; or

(b) *continue automatically,* normally until ended by *either* party on specified notice (a *rolling contract*), which gives an ongoing contract but either party the chance to exit if they want; or

(c)   *continue if both parties agree*, which really means it ends if they don't agree in time (with neither being obliged to be reasonable about agreeing or not); or

(d)   *continue if one party* (normally either but occasionally just one specified party) elects to continue, often by exercising some form of *option*. A one-way option like this needs to be watched carefully.

Rolling and evergreen contracts – If you see the relationship continuing, rolling contracts are often the best approach, so that if the parties just carry on beyond the initial term there is a contract in place. But if there is a rolling contract, make sure there's also a break clause (see below) and beware the 'evergreen' contract, which rolls forward (e.g. from year to year) or enables just one party to renew it, without any means of bringing it to an end except for the other's breach or insolvency. The disguised evergreen is one that is for a fixed period with the right to renew on the same terms. The same terms include the renewal right, so the contract again becomes potentially never-ending. You will need either to limit (e.g. to one occasion only) or exclude this renewal right altogether to avoid being forced to buy your freedom from an indefinite obligation.

10.3 How is a contract terminated when no one is in breach?

Break clauses – Rather than a renewal option, the contract may be for a longer period with the right for one or both parties to terminate on written notice for any reason at stated times.

Notice to terminate – The notice period will depend on the circumstances, with one, three and six months being common.

> Notice to terminate should normally be no shorter or longer than the time the parties need to tidy up their business arrangements under the contract and make any necessary new arrangements.

It's also important to be clear on the timescale, either the date(s) by which notice should be served or the date(s) by which notice will expire. Assume, for example, that the contract is a rolling contract which states:

> This agreement may be terminated without cause by either party by not more than six months' nor less than three months' written notice to the other expiring on or before 31 December in any year of the Term.

This means that to be effective notice must be served (in broad terms) no earlier than 1 July nor later than 30 September so as to expire on 31 December that year. This gives both parties certainty that if notice isn't given by then, the contract will run at least another year, and avoids lengthy notice periods hanging over the parties. Do also look carefully at the notices clause itself (see #9.4) to ensure that the notice complies with the timescales; to miss even by a day can bind you to another year of a contract you may no longer want.

Watch timescales – Try to negotiate a clause that's not too restrictive, and watch clauses that limit the right to narrow windows of time. For example, a clause requiring 'six months' notice expiring on [stated date]' means you'd have to give *exactly* six months' notice expiring *exactly* on that date. The wording in the example above would be safer and easier to manage.

Summary – key things to cover in notices

- the period of notice required;

- whether notice can be given by either or just one party;

- whether notice can only be given in certain circumstances (e.g. a price increase exceeding x per cent); and

- the date by which notice must be given/received or by which the notice ends.

10.4 What about breach or insolvency?

Material breach – The law generally enables one party to terminate a contract if the other breaches it in such a substantial way a) as to show no intention to honour the contract at all (also called *repudiation*) or b) the victim risks losing the essential benefits of the contract (*material breach*). Most contracts require prior notice and the chance to remedy the breach, as in the reasonably typical wording below (but see the notes).

Insolvency – The clause will also normally give one party the right to terminate immediately if the other becomes insolvent, which is often subject to a detailed legal definition (#6.8).

An example of a termination clause for material breach or insolvency

> Either party[1] may terminate this agreement immediately on written notice to the other party if the other either a) commits a material breach[2] of this agreement and, where that breach is capable of remedy, fails to remedy it within [14 days] of written notice from the non-breaching party specifying the breach and requiring it to be remedied[3]; or b) becomes insolvent [or unable to pay his or its debts as and when they fall due][4].

Notes

[1] The termination rights are mutual – not one-sided.

[2] The breach must be material – see above. A minor breach does not give the right to terminate (though it may give a right to damages – see chapter 9).

[3] If the breach is material and can be remedied, the breach notice should state that and give time for remedy. If it can't be remedied, for example because it is what the law has classified as 'irremediable', the breach notice can state that termination may take effect immediately. The time period given should be reasonable and enough to remedy likely breaches in the relevant circumstances.

[4] The insolvency clause is again short, avoiding legal complexity. The definition of 'inability to pay debts' will generally pick up any marginal cases, but could affect any business with cash-flow problems, so if you expect to be in that position you might want to vary or delete those words and add in a more formal definition.

10.5 What happens if one of the companies is taken over?

Change of control clauses – If a limited company is a contract party, control of that company can pass to someone else, typically on a *takeover* where a third party buys all or most of the shares in the company and takes over its direction. The company stays the same but there are likely to be different people (and principles) pulling the strings. One way to cover this risk is a *change of control clause*, giving the right to terminate the contract (normally on short notice) if the other party undergoes a change of control. (This may have to be reciprocal if you trade through a limited company.) In practice the same result may occur if just the management changes, but that is much harder to provide for. Many definitions of control incorporate complex statutory definitions, so the example below uses a very simple definition of 'control' and also gives a limited period of time for the 'innocent' party to make up its mind whether it will be adversely affected or not.

Defined term

Control – The right to direct the affairs of a company at shareholder or management level.

Termination clause – Either party may terminate this agreement immediately on [at least one month's] written notice to the other within [three] months of first becoming aware that the other party has undergone a change of Control.

10.6 What if someone dies?

When the owner of a business dies:

- If the business is a limited company, the contract remains in force;

- If the owner is sole proprietor, the contract will pass to the personal representatives;

- In either case if the death means that the business cannot carry on as planned, the contract may end by *frustration*, meaning that the original purpose becomes impossible to achieve because of the death. There then needs to be a final reckoning up to that point.

- If the death does not prevent the contract continuing to be performed, it will continue with the personal representatives taking the place of the deceased.

> By way of example, a normal publishing contract will probably be frustrated if the author dies before finishing the book, but not after the book has been delivered in final form if the author has fully performed and the estate can receive the royalties.

10.7 What happens after the contract ends?

The principles – As well as thinking about *how to terminate* it's wise to consider *what should happen afterwards*, and whether this is different between fault and no-fault termination. For example, you might want to prevent a former distributor from continuing to sell your stock after termination if this were likely to affect sales by a new distributor. Or you might want to limit this right to a stated period after termination, and even to negotiate the right to buy back excess stock after that at cost or agreed discount. They in turn might want this repurchase to be an obligation on your part, something you probably wouldn't want to agree if you terminated because they were in breach. Consider therefore what provisions should be added to protect your position after termination. These might include restrictions against future competition (#8.3).

10.8 What happens to employees on termination of a contract?

With agreements for services, as seen at #5.8, there is always the possibility that any employees involved wholly or mainly in the contract work will transfer automatically under the TUPE regulations. This possibility arises both at the start and end of an outsourcing project, for example, in relation to any job roles that are essentially replicated when the work goes out-of-house or comes back in again. The cost and risk of TUPE compliance may be considerable, so these possibilities need to be considered and covered in the contract at the outset.

10.9 How do I best handle termination?

Thinking it through – Just because you have a contract with the right to terminate on breach does not mean that it is the most sensible thing to do. There may still be a beneficial relationship to continue if confidence can be restored and, if appropriate, suitable compensation agreed. But if there is a material breach (or series of breaches which might together make up a material breach) and confidence is totally lost, there may be no point in soldiering on.

Managing the emotion – No one likes to be accused of breach; those accused tend to become highly defensive and emotions can run high. So it pays to recognise your own emotional reaction, act as dispassionately as possible, seek early professional advice and remain open to a sensible resolution. Above all, don't at this stage (or any stage) make allegations you can't prove!

> This is the time to stand back and look carefully at the options; it may also be time to swallow your pride and renegotiate in the interests of the longer term. Small businesses can rarely afford to get involved in big disputes and sometimes it may be better to call it quits and walk away until you are strong enough to fight the heavyweights.

SUMMARY
10 Point Checklist

Here's a final checklist, cross-referred to the 10 chapters:

1. You have an agreement containing all the legal essentials. ☑

2. You have thought through and covered off projected benefits, costs and risks. ☑

3. All terms are set out in writing in a way that makes sense to all. ☑

4. Any goods are clearly described so that you'll know they meet expectations. ☑

5. Any services are adequately specified so you'll know they are up to standard. ☑

6. All relevant payment and financial terms have been included. ☑

7. Confidentiality, copyright and other IPR in anything used or developed is covered. ☑

8. Suitable warranties, indemnities, restrictions and exemptions cover the main risk areas. ☑

9. You have the most relevant boilerplate clauses and have diarised key dates. ☑

10. You know when and how the contract may be ended. ☑

The rest is up to you!

Further reference

UK websites

(Note: although not definitive, these official websites are good reference points, but especially if you use search engines, take care to ensure you are reading their most up-to-date content.)

Companies House (**www.companieshouse.gov.uk**)

Sales to consumers – OFT (**www.oft.gov.uk**) / Department for Business Innovation and Skills (**www.bis.gov.uk**)

Taxation – HMRC (**www.hmrc.gov.uk**)

Intellectual property – Intellectual Property Office (**www.ipo.gov.uk**) and worldwide (**www.wipo.int**)

Data protection / personal information – Information Commissioner's Office (**www.ico.gov.uk**)

Escrow agreements – NCC (**www.nccgroup.com**)

CISG – Contracts for the sale of international goods (**www.cisg.law.pace.edu**)

NCC Group – source code escrow arrangements (**www.nccgroup.com**)

For a more in-depth view of business contracts you may wish to read the author's *Business Contracts Handbook*, published by Ashgate/Gower (**tinyurl.com/ce5z34o**)

Acknowledgements

My thanks go to all those who have helped in various ways to bring this book into being, and specifically Emma Jones who made the connection, Louise Hinchen who followed up, Kathy Oldridge, Vanessa Milton and my son, Sam, who all provided business, legal and tax input and especially Tracey Petter of SNR Denton for her detailed review and comments.

Index

(Numbers in bold type indicate
sample contract wording for the
issue in question.)

A

act of God *see force majeure*
agency/agent 56–59, 71, 137
appendix, to agreement *see*
  schedule
arbitration, and dispute resolution
  69, 151
assignment (of contracts) 70, 81,
  142–3, 144
attorney, power of 15
audit rights 100
author contracts *see also*
  copyright, publishing contracts
authority
    actual/apparent/warranty of 29,
    37, 111, **130**
avoidance of doubt 41

B

bankruptcy *see* insolvency
battle of the forms 47, 49
benefit (and burden) of contract 19,
  143
boilerplate clauses **144–9**
breach, of contract 42, 51, 79, 84,
  131–2, 141–2, 145, 149–51, 159, **160**,
  163
break clause 157
B2B/B2C 45, 53, 60, 96, 133
business efficacy 11

C

cancellation 62, 85–6, **88**, **90**, 96
certainty, of contract 9–11, 67
change, of control 80, 102, 144,
  160–1
changes, in contract *see* variation
child/children 29, 61
choice of law 147–8
CISG 4
claims handling **130–1**
Companies Registry 36, 169
company, limited *see* limited
  company
company search 36
competition law 135–7, 148
computer programs, services,
  systems, contracts *see* technology
    contracts
conditions of business *see* terms of
  business
confidentiality/confidential
  information 20, 38, 71, **76**, 80, 83, 86,
    88–9, 108–11, 120, 126, 129
consequential loss 132–3, **55**, **78**, **91**
consideration 9, 12, 15, 113, 141
construction (of contracts) *see*
  interpreting (contracts)
consultancy 113
consumer contracts 12, 14, 45, 46, 57,
  60, 62, 96, 126, 133, 136, 148
contract essentials 9, 39
control *see* change of control
conventions used in book 34
copyright 14, 38, 77, **79**, 86, 99, 108,
  110–5, 117, 120–2

counter-offer *see* offer
course of dealing 11, 48
credit 54, 97–8, 100–1
custom and practice 11

D

damages 27–8, 42, 79, 130–1, 132,
    149–51, 160
databases /database rights 77, 115
data protection (*see also* privacy) 62,
    116, 120, 169
date, of documents 33, 34–5, 155–6
deal memo 21, 23, 24
death 55, 78, 121, 133, 143, 161–2
deed 12, 15, 143
default *see* breach
defective contracts 11, 330
defined terms 34, 37, 76, 128
delay 51, 53, 80–1, 142, 147–8
delivery
    deed *see* deed
    goods/products *see* goods
design rights 113, 115
direct/indirect loss 55, 78, 90, 132
disputes 14, 27, 37, 33, 50, 68–9, 117–9,
    150, 163
distributor 52, 56–9, 162
draft contract 23
D2C 45, 46

E

email 2, 14, 18, 22, 28, 62, 80, 82,
    144–5
employment/employees 5, 15, 65,
    68–71, 73–4, 115
    see also transfer regulations
    tax issues 69
endeavours, best or reasonable 41,
    77, 81, 85, 88, 147
English law 4, 81, 132

entire agreement clause 80, 133, 145–6
escrow 35, 119, 167
EULA 119
European law 4
event planning contracts 85–91
exclusivity 26, 59, 70, 113, 118, 120–1,
    135
exemption, incl. exclusion and
    limitation, clauses 46, 119, 125,
    130–135
export (trading abroad) *see*
    international

F

force majeure 119, 134, 146–7
fraud/fraudulent action 55, 78, 134
frustration, of contract 161

G

gentlemen's agreement 13
good faith 40–1, 61
goods/products
    defective 47, 51, 54, 62, 135
    delivery 11, 38, 47–51, 52–4, 62,
        95, 99
    description 37–8, 46, 50
    distinguished from services 45
    fitness for purpose/quality 46, 51
    inspection 50–52, 54
    risk in 52
    safety 62, 122, 126, 148
    title in 46, 52
guarantee, financial 101, 102

H

hardcore terms/restrictions 136, 151–
    60

I

ideas 108, 112, 115
identity 28, 142, **148**
illegality 29, 81
implied terms 11–2, 45–6, 49, 68, **80**, 113, **146**
indemnity 42, 58, 70, **78**, 89, **91**, 122, 129–31, **146**
insolvency 47, 52, **54, 55, 79, 84**, 99, 102–4, 119, 155, 157, 159–60
insurance/insurers 20, 52, 100, 133–5
intellectual property (IP) 14, 26, 71, 107–14
interest (on debt) 98
international dealings 4, 46, 50–1, 147
interpreting/interpretation ('construction') of contracts 41, 76, 132–3
invitation to tender (ITT) 72

J

joint and several liability 42
jumping the gun 25
jurisdiction/jurisdiction clauses 81, 112, **147–8**

K

know-how 115, 126
KPIs 39, 66, 68, 72

L

land, contracts relating to 14, 15
language of contracts 33, 60
legal commitment 12, 13, 15
letter of intent (LOI) 27, 40

limitation clauses *see* exemption clauses
limited companies/limited liability partnerships (LLPs) 35, 60, 101, 122
liquidated damages 150–1
liquidation/liquidator *see* insolvency
literary works *see* publishing
loss 42, 51–3, 55, 78–9, 91, 130, 131–5, 137, 150–1

M

market share 136
material breach 51, **79, 84**, 118, 151, 159, **160**, 163
meetings 2, 14, 22, 62, 109
misrepresentation 28, 134, 145, **146**
mistakes 27–8, 36, 150
mitigation of loss 151
moral rights 115

N

negligence **55, 78, 89**, 121, 133, 137
negotiating contracts 19, 23
non-compete clauses *see* restrictive covenants
non-reliance clause **80**, 91, 133, **146**
notice/notices clause 53, **79–82**, 144–5, 155–9
novation 143

O

offer, counter-offer and acceptance 9, 10, 22, 49, 60–1, 116, 150
Office of Fair Trading (OFT) 61, 169
outsourcing 72–4, 163

P

parties, to a contract 33, 35, 36
patents 77, 114, 117
payment 9, 26, 68, 69, 97–9
penalty/penalty clause *see* liquidated damages
personal contracts 70
phone calls 14, 22
preliminary clauses 33, 37, 51
previous dealings 11, 48
price 1,2, 9–12, 38, 40, 50, 54, 57, 61, 68–9, 95–6, 136–7
privacy 62, 86, 115–6, 120
products *see* goods
profit(s), loss of, claims 134–5
publishing contracts (including literary work) 99–100, 112, 162
punctuation 33

R

reasonableness 41, 127
recitals *see* preliminary clauses
rectification 28
rejection, of goods 51
remedy 53, 54, 79, 84, 98, 134, 150, 159–60
representation (*see also* misrepresentation) 42
repudiation 150
resale price/RPM 56–7, 136
restrictive covenants/non-compete 71, 111, 115, 121–2, 126, 127–9, 135
retention of title (ROT) 52, 103
risk, in contracts 20, 25, 26, 58, 101, 122–5
royalties 99

S

Sale of Goods Act 46
schedules/appendices 149
service levels/quality 65, 118
services, contracts for 75–82, 82–5
set-off 99
severance 148
sign/signature 2, 14–5, 27, 29, 34, 37, 39, 40, 82, 85, 87, 110
software *see* computer systems
sole remedy clause 53–4, 134
sole rights 59
sub-contract 70, 81, 143
subject to contract 21–2, 26–7, 150
subrogation 135

T

technology contracts 9, 45, 75–82, 82–5, 107–8, 115–6, 117–9, 121, 126, 130–1, 143
terminating contracts/termination generally 58, 155–7, 160–2
terms (and conditions/of business TOB), etc. 40, 46–8, 53–6
third party rights 149
time of the essence 51,53
title *see* goods
trademark 114
Transfer of Undertakings (Protection of Employment) Regulations (TUPE) 59, 73–4, 162–3
transfer of contracts *see* assignment

U

unfair commercial practice 61
unfair contract terms 6, 48, 133
unfair trading 61

unreasonably withheld (consent
  not to be) 41, **81**, 130, **142**
US/USA 4, 41, 96, 103, 112, 116, 136
UNCITRAL 4

V

variations (to a contract) 81, 96, 142,
  148–9
VAT/sales taxes 20, 25, **38**, 45, 54, 70,
  78, 83, 90, 96
voluntary arrangement *see*
  insolvency
vulnerable customers 61

W

waiver 81, 148
warranty 37, 42, 66, 70, **79**, **89**, 114,
  130–1, 129–31
websites 47, 48, 60–2
without prejudice 21, 150
witness, need for 15, 39
written contracts, need for 14, 22–3, 25

BlackBerry

With a BlackBerry® in hand, you have business at your fingertips.

With BlackBerry there is so much you can do:

Work anywhere

- BlackBerry 'push' technology delivers emails wherever you are
- Keep up to date with email, calendar entries, contacts, tasks and memos

Communicate anytime

- BBM™ (BlackBerry® Messenger) – the cost-effective way to keep your business moving
- 'D' and 'R' appear so you know when your message has been delivered and read

Instant access

- With BlackBerry App World™ you can easily get the right apps to help you get the right information, be more productive, responsive and efficient.

Manage your business

- Keep on top of your businesses cash flow, using one of the financial apps to assist you
- Enjoy peace of mind knowing BlackBerry® smartphones have the highest levels of security

BlackBerry® smartphones and solutions are 'built for business', but you can also have fun with a BlackBerry® smartphone. Access the best social networking sites, thousands of apps and great multimedia functions. Check out more on BlackBerry.com and join My BlackBerry to get all the latest news and offers.

www.BlackBerry.co.uk
www.BlackBerry.co.uk/sme
www.twitter.com/BlackBerry

About Brightword Publishing

Brightword publishing is a new venture from Harriman House and Enterprise Nation. Brightword produce print books, kits and digital products aimed at a small business and start up audience, providing high-quality information from high profile experts in an accessible and approachable way.

Our Other Business Bites

Twitter Your Business

By Mark Shaw
eBook ISBN: 978-1-90800-304-1
Print ISBN: 978-1-908003-18-8

Selling for Small Business

By Jackie Wade
eBook ISBN: 978-1-90800-308-9
Print ISBN: 978-1-908003-19-5

Finance for Small Business

By Emily Coltman
eBook ISBN: 978-1-90800-306-5
Print ISBN: 978-1-908003-20-1

The Small Business Guide to China

By David Howell
eBook ISBN: 978-1-908003-11-9
Print ISBN: 978-1-908003-22-5

Other Products from Brightword

49 Quick Ways to Market your Business for Free

By Sarah-Jane White
eBook ISBN: 978-0-85719-144-1

50 Fantastic Franchises!

By Emma Jones and Sarah Clay
eBook ISBN: 978-1-90800-302-7

Go Global: How to Take Your Business to the World

By Emma Jones
Print ISBN: 978-1-90800-300-3
eBook ISBN: 978-1-90800-303-4

Motivating Business Mums

By Debbie O'Connor
eBook ISBN: 978-1-90800-309-6

The Start-Up Kit: Everything you need to know to start a small business

By Emma Jones
ISBN: 978-1-90800-301-0

Lightning Source UK Ltd.
Milton Keynes UK
UKOW04f1333250813

215931UK00005B/16/P

9 781908 003218